D0966149

ALEXANDER POPE

BY

LESLIE STEPHEN

AMS PRESS
NEW YORK

Reprinted from the edition of 1888, London
First AMS EDITION published 1968
Manufactured in the United States of America

Library of Congress Catalogue Card Number: 68-58397

AMS PRESS, INC.
New York, N.Y. 10003

PREFATORY NOTE.

THE life and writings of Pope have been discussed in a literature more voluminous than that which exists in the case of almost any other English man of letters. No biographer, however, has produced a definitive or exhaustive work. It seems therefore desirable to indicate the main authorities upon which such a biographer would have to rely, and which have been consulted for the purpose of the following necessarily brief and imperfect sketch.

The first life of Pope was a catchpenny book, by William Ayre, published in 1745, and remarkable chiefly as giving the first version of some demonstrably erroneous statements, unfortunately adopted by later writers. In 1751, Warburton, as Pope's literary executor, published the authoritative edition of the poet's works, with notes containing some biographical matter. In 1769 appeared a life by Owen Ruffhead, who wrote under Warburton's inspiration. This is a dull and meagre performance, and much of it is devoted to an attack—partly written by Warburton himself—upon the criticisms advanced in the first volume of Joseph Warton's Essay on Pope. Warton's first volume was published in 1756; and it seems that the dread of Warburton's wrath counted for something in the delay of the second volume, which did not appear till 1782. The Essay contains a good many anecdotes of interest. Warton's edition of Pope—the notes in which are chiefly drawn from the Essay—was published in 1797. The Life by Johnson appeared in 1781; it is

admirable in many ways; but Johnson had taken the
least possible trouble in ascertaining facts.   Both Warton
and Johnson had before them the manuscript collections
of Joseph Spence, who had known Pope personally
during the last twenty years of his life, and wanted
nothing but literary ability to have become an efficient
Boswell.   Spence's anecdotes, which were not published
till 1820, give the best obtainable information upon many
points, especially in regard to Pope's childhood.   This
ends the list of biographers who were in any sense contemporary with Pope.   Their statements must be checked and
supplemented by the poet's own letters, and innumerable
references to him in the literature of the time.   In 1806
appeared the edition of Pope by Bowles, with a life pre-
fixed. Bowles expressed an unfavourable opinion of many
points in Pope's character, and some remarks by Campbell, in his specimens of English poets, led to a controversy (1819—1826) in which Bowles defended his
views against Campbell, Byron, Roscoe, and others, and
which incidentally cleared up some disputed questions.
Roscoe, the author of the Life of Leo X., published his
edition of Pope in 1824.   A life is contained in the first
volume, but it is a feeble performance; and the notes,
many of them directed against Bowles, are of little value.
A more complete biography was published by R. Carruthers (with an edition of the works), in 1854.   The
second, and much improved, edition appeared in 1857,
and is still the most convenient life of Pope, though Mr.
Carruthers was not fully acquainted with the last results
of some recent investigations, which have thrown a new
light upon the poet's career.

The writer who took the lead in these inquiries was
the late Mr. Dilke.   Mr. Dilke published the results of
his investigations (which were partly guided by the
discovery of a previously unpublished correspondence
between Pope and his friend Caryll), in the *Athenæum*
and *Notes and Queries*, at various intervals, from 1854 to
1860.   His contributions to the subject have been col-
lated in the first volume of the *Papers of a Critic*,

edited by his grandson, the present Sir Charles W. Dilke, in 1875. Meanwhile Mr. Croker had been making an extensive collection of materials for an exhaustive edition of Pope's works, in which he was to be assisted by Mr. Peter Cunningham. After Croker's death these materials were submitted by Mr. Murray to Mr. Whitwell Elwin, whose own researches have greatly extended our knowledge, and who had also the advantage of Mr. Dilke's advice. Mr. Elwin began, in 1871, the publication of the long-promised edition. It was to have occupied ten volumes—five of poems and five of correspondence, the latter of which was to include a very large proportion of previously unpublished matter. Unfortunately for all students of English literature, only two volumes of poetry and three of correspondence have appeared. The notes and prefaces, however, contain a vast amount of information, which clears up many previously disputed points in the poet's career; and it is to be hoped that the materials collected for the remaining volumes will not be ultimately lost. It is easy to dispute some of Mr. Elwin's critical opinions, but it would be impossible to speak too highly of the value of his investigations of facts. Without a study of his work, no adequate knowledge of Pope is attainable.

The ideal biographer of Pope, if he ever appears, must be endowed with the qualities of an acute critic and a patient antiquarian; and it would take years of labour to work out all the minute problems connected with the subject. All that I can profess to have done is to have given a short summary of the obvious facts, and of the main conclusions established by the evidence given at length in the writings of Mr. Dilke and Mr. Elwin. I have added such criticisms as seemed desirable in a work of this kind, and I must beg pardon by anticipation if I have fallen into inaccuracies in relating a story so full of pitfalls for the unwary.

L. S.

CONTENTS.

POPE.

CHAPTER I.

EARLY YEARS.

THE father of Alexander Pope was a London merchant, a devout Catholic, and not improbably a convert to Catholicism. His mother was one of seventeen children of William Turner, of York; one of her sisters was the wife of Cooper, the well-known portrait-painter. Mrs. Cooper was the poet's godmother; she died when he was five years old, leaving to her sister, Mrs. Pope, a "grinding-stone and muller," and their mother's "picture in limning;" and to her nephew, the little Alexander, all her "books, pictures, and medals set in gold or otherwise."

In after-life the poet made some progress in acquiring the art of painting; and the bequest suggests the possibility that the precocious child had already given some indications of artistic taste. Affectionate eyes were certainly on the watch for any symptoms of developing talent. Pope was born on May 21st, 1688—the *annus mirabilis* which introduced a new political era in England, and was fatal to the hopes of ardent Catholics. About the same

B

time, partly, perhaps, in consequence of the catastrophe,
Pope's father retired from business, and settled at
Binfield—a village two miles from Wokingham and nine
from Windsor. It is near Bracknell, one of Shelley's
brief perching places, and in such a region as poets might
love, if poetic praises of rustic seclusion are to be taken
seriously. To the east were the "forests and green
retreats" of Windsor, and the wild heaths of Bagshot,
Chobham and Aldershot stretched for miles to the South.
Some twelve miles off in that direction, one may remark,
lay Moor Park, where the sturdy pedestrian, Swift, was
living with Sir W. Temple during great part of Pope's
childhood; but it does not appear that his walks ever
took him to Pope's neighbourhood, nor did he see, till
some years later, the lad with whom he was to form one
of the most famous of literary friendships. The little
household was presumably a very quiet one, and remained
fixed at Binfield for twenty-seven years, till the son had
grown to manhood and celebrity. From the earliest
period he seems to have been a domestic idol. He was
not an only child, for he had a half-sister by his father's
side, who must have been considerably older than himself,
as her mother died nine years before the poet's birth. But
he was the only child of his mother, and his parents concentrated upon him an affection which he returned with
touching ardour and persistence. They were both forty-
six in the year of his birth. He inherited headaches from
his mother, and a crooked figure from his father. A
nurse who shared their care, lived with him for many
years, and was buried by him, with an affectionate
epitaph, in 1725. The family tradition represents him as
a sweet-tempered child, and says that he was called the
" little nightingale," from the beauty of his voice. As the

sickly, solitary, and precocious infant of elderly parents, we may guess that he was not a little spoilt, if only in the technical sense.

The religion of the family made their seclusion from the world the more rigid, and by consequence must have strengthened their mutual adhesiveness. Catholics were then harassed by a legislation which would be condemned by any modern standard as intolerably tyrannical. Whatever apology may be urged for the legislators on the score of contemporary prejudices or special circumstances, their best excuse is that their laws were rather intended to satisfy constituents, and to supply a potential means of defence, than to be carried into actual execution. It does not appear that the Popes had to fear any active molestation in the quiet observance of their religious duties. Yet a Catholic was not only a member of a hated minority, regarded by the rest of his countrymen as representing the evil principle in politics and religion, but was rigorously excluded from a public career, and from every position of honour or authority. In times of excitement the severer laws might be put in force. The public exercise of the Catholic religion was forbidden, and to be a Catholic was to be predisposed to the various Jacobite intrigues which still had many chances in their favour. When the pretender was expected in 1744, a proclamation, to which Pope thought it decent to pay obedience, forbade the appearance of Catholics within ten miles of London; and in 1730 we find him making interest on behalf of a nephew, who had been prevented from becoming an attorney because the judges were rigidly enforcing the oaths of supremacy and allegiance.

Catholics had to pay double taxes and were prohibited from acquiring real property. The elder Pope, according

to a certainly inaccurate story, had a conscientious objection to investing his money in the funds of a Protestant
government, and, therefore, having converted his capital
into coin, put it in a strong-box, and took it out as he
wanted it. The old merchant was not quite so helpless,
for we know that he had investments in the French
rentes, besides other sources of income; but the story
probably reflects the fact that his religious disqualifications
hampered even his financial position..

Pope's character was affected in many ways by the fact
of his belonging to a sect thus harassed and restrained.
Persecution, like bodily infirmity, has an ambiguous
influence. If it sometimes generates in its victims a heroic
hatred of oppression, it sometimes predisposes them to
the use of the weapons of intrigue and falsehood, by
which the weak evade the tyranny of the strong. If
under that discipline Pope learnt to love toleration, he
was not untouched by the more demoralizing influences
of a life passed in an atmosphere of incessant plotting
and evasion. A more direct consequence was his ex-
clusion from the ordinary schools. The spirit of the
rickety lad might have been broken by the rough
training of Eton or Westminster in those days; as, on
the other hand, he might have profited by acquiring a
livelier perception of the meaning of that virtue of fair-
play, the appreciation of which is held to be a set-off
against the brutalizing influences of our system of
public education. As it was, Pope was condemned to a
desultory education. He picked up some rudiments of
learning from the family priest; he was sent to a school
at Twyford, where he is said to have got into trouble
for writing a lampoon upon his master; he went for a
short time to another in London, where he gave a more

creditable if less characteristic proof of his poetical precocity. Like other lads of genius, he put together a kind
of play—a combination, it seems, of the speeches in
Ogilby's Iliad—and got it acted by his schoolfellows.
These brief snatches of schooling, however, counted
for little. Pope settled at home at the early age of
twelve, and plunged into the delights of miscellaneous
reading with the ardour of precocious talent. He read
so eagerly that his feeble constitution threatened to
break down, and when about seventeen, he despaired of
recovery, and wrote a farewell to his friends. One of
them, an Abbé Southcote, applied for advice to the celebrated Dr. Radcliffe, who judiciously prescribed idleness
and exercise. Pope soon recovered, and, it is pleasant to
add, showed his gratitude long afterwards by obtaining for
Southcote, through Sir Robert Walpole, a desirable piece
of French preferment. Self-guided studies have their
advantages, as Pope himself observed, but they do not
lead a youth through the dry places of literature, or
stimulate him to severe intellectual training. Pope seems
to have made some hasty raids into philosophy and
theology; he dipped into Locke, and found him
"insipid;" he went through a collection of the contro-
versial literature of the reign of James II., which seems to
have constituted the paternal library, and was alternately
Protestant and Catholic, according to the last book which
he had read. But it was upon poetry and pure literature
that he flung himself with a genuine appetite. He learnt
languages to get at the story, unless a translation offered
an easier path, and followed wherever fancy led "like a
boy gathering flowers in the fields and woods."

It is needless to say that he never became a scholar in
the strict sense of the term. Voltaire declared that he

could hardly read or speak a word of French; and his knowledge of Greek would have satisfied Bentley as little as his French satisfied Voltaire. Yet he must have been fairly conversant with the best known French literature of the time, and he could probably stumble through Homer with the help of a crib and a guess at the general meaning. He says himself that at this early period, he went through all the best critics; all the French, English and Latin poems of any name; " Homer and some of the greater Greek poets in the original," and Tasso and Ariosto in translations.

Pope at any rate acquired a wide knowledge of English poetry. Waller, Spenser, and Dryden were, he says, his great favourites in the order named, till he was twelve. Like so many other poets, he took, infinite delight in the *Faery Queen ;* but Dryden, the great poetical luminary of his own day, naturally exercised a predominant influence upon his mind. He declared that he had learnt versification wholly from Dryden's works, and always mentioned his name with reverence. Many scattered remarks reported by Spence, and the still more conclusive evidence of frequent appropriation, show him to have been familiar with the poetry of the preceding century, and with much that had gone out of fashion in his time, to a degree in which he was probably excelled by none of his successors, with the exception of Gray. Like Gray he contemplated at one time the history of English poetry which was in some sense executed by Warton. It is characteristic, too, that he early showed a critical spirit. From a boy, he says, he could distinguish between sweetness and softness of numbers, Dryden exemplifying softness and Waller sweetness ; and the remark, whatever its value, shows that he had been analysing his impressions and reflecting upon the technical secrets of his art.

Such study naturally suggests the trembling aspiration, " I, too, am a poet." Pope adopts with apparent sincerity the Ovidian phrase,

> As yet a child, nor yet a fool to fame
> I lisp'd in numbers, for the numbers came.

His father corrected his early performances and when not satisfied, sent him back with the phrase, "These are not good rhymes." He translated any passages that struck him in his reading, excited by the examples of Ogilby's Homer and Sandys' Ovid. His boyish ambition prompted him before he was fifteen to attempt an epic poem ; the subject was Alcander, Prince of Rhodes, driven from his home by Deucalion, father of Minos ; and the work was modestly intended to emulate in different passages the beauties of Milton, Cowley, Spenser, Statius, Homer, Virgil, Ovid, and Claudian. Four books of this poem survived for a long time, for Pope had a more than parental fondness for all the children of his brain, and always had an eye to possible reproduction. Scraps from this early epic were worked into the Essay on Criticism and the Dunciad. This couplet, for example, from the last work comes straight, we are told, from Alcander,—

> As man's Mæanders to the vital spring
> Roll all their tides, then back their circles bring.

Another couplet, preserved by Spence, will give a sufficient taste of its quality :—

> Shields, helms, and swords all jangle as they hang,
> And sound formidinous with angry clang.

After this we shall hardly censure Atterbury for approving (perhaps suggesting) its destruction in later years. Pope long meditated another epic, relating the foundation of the English government by Brutus of Troy, with a superabundant display of didactic morality and religion. Happily this dreary conception, though it occupied much thought, never came to the birth.

The time soon came when these tentative flights were to be superseded by more serious efforts. Pope's ambition was directed into the same channel by his innate propensities and by the accidents of his position. No man ever displayed a more exclusive devotion to literature, or was more tremblingly sensitive to the charm of literary glory. His zeal was never distracted by any rival emotion. Almost from his cradle to his grave his eye was fixed unremittingly upon the sole purpose of his life. The whole energies of his mind were absorbed in the struggle to place his name as high as possible in that temple of fame, which he painted after Chaucer in one of his early poems. External conditions pointed to letters as the sole path to eminence, but it was precisely the path for which he had admirable qualifications. The sickly son of the Popish tradesman was cut off from the bar, the senate, and the church. Physically contemptible, politically ostracized, and in a humble social position, he could yet win this dazzling prize and force his way with his pen to the highest pinnacle of contemporary fame. Without adventitious favour and in spite of many bitter antipathies, he was to become the acknowledged head of English literature, and the welcome companion of all the most eminent men of his time. Though he could not foresee his career from the start, he worked as vigorously as if the goal had already been in sight ; and each successive victory in the field of letters was realized the more keenly from his sense of the disadvantages in face of which it had been won. In tracing his rapid ascent,

we shall certainly find reason to doubt his proud assertion,—

  That, if he pleased, he pleased by manly ways,

but it is impossible for any lover of literature to grudge
admiration to this singular triumph of pure intellect over
external disadvantages, and the still more depressing influences of incessant physical suffering.

Pope had indeed certain special advantages which he
was not slow in turning to account. In one respect
even his religion helped him to emerge into fame.
There was naturally a certain free-masonry amongst the
Catholics allied by fellow-feeling under the general
antipathy. The relations between Pope and his co-
religionists exercised a material influence upon his later
life. Within a few miles of Binfield lived the Blounts
of Mapledurham, a fine old Elizabethan mansion on
the banks of the Thames, near Reading, which had
been held by a royalist Blount in the civil war against
a parliamentary assault. It was a more interesting
circumstance to Pope that Mr. Lister Blount, the then
representative of the family, had two fair daughters,
Teresa and Martha, of about the poet's age. Another of
Pope's Catholic acquaintances was John Caryll, of West
Grinstead in Sussex, nephew of a Caryll who had been
the representative of James II. at the Court of Rome,
and who, following his master into exile, received the
honours of a titular peerage and held office in the melancholy court of the Pretender. In such circles Pope
might have been expected to imbibe a Jacobite and
Catholic horror of Whigs and freethinkers. In fact,
however, he belonged from his youth to the followers of
Gallio, and seems to have paid to religious duties just as

much attention as would satisfy his parents. His mind
was really given to literature ; and he found his earliest
patron in his immediate neighbourhood.   This was Sir
W. Trumbull, who had retired to his native village of
Easthampstead in 1697, after being ambassador at the
Porte under James II., and Secretary of State under
William III.   Sir William made acquaintance with the
Popes, praised the father's artichokes, and was delighted
with the precocious son.   The old diplomatist and the
young poet soon became fast friends, took constant rides
together, and talked over classic and modern poetry.
Pope made Trumbull acquainted with Milton's juvenile
poems, and Trumbull encouraged Pope to follow in
Milton's steps.   He gave, it seems, the first suggestion to
Pope that he should translate Homer ; and he exhorted
his young friend to preserve his health by flying from
tavern company—*tanquam ex incendio.*   Another early
patron was William Walsh, a Worcestershire country
gentleman of fortune and fashion, who condescended
to dabble in poetry after the manner of Waller, and
to write remonstrances upon Celia's cruelty, verses to
his mistress against marriage, epigrams, and pastoral
eclogues.   He was better known, however, as a critic, and
had been declared by Dryden to be, without flattery,
the best in the nation.   Pope received from him one
piece of advice which has become famous.   We had had
great poets—so said the " knowing Walsh," as Pope
calls him—" but never one great poet that was correct ;"
and he accordingly recommended Pope to make correctness his great aim.   The advice doubtless impressed the
young man as the echo of his own convictions.   Walsh
died (1708), before the effect of his suggestion had become
fully perceptible.

The acquaintance with Walsh was due to Wycherley,
who had submitted Pope's Pastorals to his recognized
critical authority.   Pope's intercourse with Wycherley
and another early friend, Henry Cromwell, had a more
important bearing upon his early career.   He kept up
a correspondence with each of these friends, whilst he was
still passing through his probationary period ; and the
letters published long afterwards under singular circum-
stances to be hereafter related, give the fullest revelation
of his character and position at this time.   Both Wycherley and Cromwell were known to the Englefields of
Whiteknights, near Reading, a Catholic family, in
which Pope first made the acquaintance of Martha
Blount, whose mother was a daughter of the old Mr.
Englefield of the day.   It was possibly, therefore, through
this connexion that Pope owed his first introduction to
the literary circles of London.   Pope, already thirsting
for literary fame, was delighted to form a connexion
which must have been far from satisfactory to his in-
dulgent parents, if they understood the character of his
new associates.

Henry Cromwell, a remote cousin of the Protector, is
known to other than minute investigators of contemporary literature by nothing except his friendship with Pope.
He was nearly thirty years older than Pope, and though
heir to an estate in the country, was at this time a gay,
though rather elderly, man about town.   Vague intima-
tions are preserved of his personal appearance.   Gay calls
him " honest hatless Cromwell with red breeches ;" and
Johnson could learn about him the single fact that he
used to ride a-hunting in a tie-wig.   The interpretation
of these outward signs may not be very obvious to modern
readers ; but it is plain from other indications that he was

one of the frequenters of coffee-houses, aimed at being
something of a rake and a wit, was on speaking terms with
Dryden, and familiar with the smaller celebrities of literature, a regular attendant at theatres, a friend of actresses,
and able to present himself in fashionable circles and
devote complimentary verses to the reigning beauties at
the Bath. When he studied the *Spectator* he might recognize some of his features reflected in the portrait of Will
Honeycomb. Pope was proud enough for the moment at
being taken by the hand by this elderly buck, though, as
Pope himself rose in the literary scale and could estimate
literary reputations more accurately, he became, it would
seem, a little ashamed of his early enthusiasm, and, at
any rate, the friendship dropped. The letters which
passed between the pair during four or five years down
to the end of 1711, show Pope in his earliest manhood. They are characteristic of that period of development in which a youth of literary genius takes literary
fame in the most desperately serious sense. Pope is evidently putting his best foot forward, and never for a moment
forgets that he is a young author writing to a recognized
critic—except, indeed, when he takes the airs of an experienced rake. We might speak of the absurd affectation
displayed in the letters, were it not that such affectation
is the most genuine nature in a clever boy. Unluckily it
became so ingrained in Pope as to survive his youthful
follies. Pope complacently indulges in elaborate paradoxes
and epigrams of the conventional epistolary style; he is
painfully anxious to be alternately sparkling and playful;
his head must be full of literature; he indulges in an
elaborate criticism of Statius, and points out what a sudden fall that author makes at one place from extravagant
bombast; he communicates the latest efforts of his muse,

and tries, one regrets to say, to get more credit for precocity
and originality than fairly belongs to him; he acciden-
tally alludes to his dog that he may bring in a translation
from the Odyssey, quote Plutarch, and introduce an
anecdote which he has heard from Trumbull about
Charles I.; he elaborately discusses Cromwell's classical translations, adduces authorities, ventures to censure
Mr. Rowe's amplifications of Lucan, and, in this respect,
thinks that Brebœuf, the famous French translator, is
equally a sinner, and writes a long letter as to the proper
use of the cæsura and the hiatus in English verse. There
are signs that the mutual criticisms became a little trying to the tempers of the correspondents. Pope seems
to be inclined to ridicule Cromwell's pedantry, and when
he affects satisfaction at learning that Cromwell has
detected him in appropriating a rondeau from Voiture,
we feel that the tension is becoming serious. Probably
he found out that Cromwell was not only a bit of a prig,
but a person not likely to reflect much glory upon his
friends, and the correspondence came to an end, when
Pope found a better market for his wares.

Pope speaks more than once in these letters of his
country retirement, where he could enjoy the company of
the muses, but where, on the other hand, he was forced
to be grave and godly, instead of drunk and scandalous as he could be in town. The jolly hunting and
drinking squires round Binfield thought him, he says, a
well-disposed person, but unluckily disqualified for their
rough modes of enjoyment by his sickly health. With
them he has not been able to make one Latin quotation,
but has learnt a song of Tom Durfey's, the sole representative of literature, it appears, at the "toping-tables"
of these thick-witted fox-hunters. Pope naturally longed

for the more refined or at least more fashionable indul-
gences of London life. Beside the literary affectation, he
sometimes adopts the more offensive affectation—unfortunately not peculiar to any period—of the youth who
wishes to pass himself off as deep in the knowledge of the
world. Pope, as may be here said once for all, could be
at times grossly indecent; and in these letters there are
passages offensive upon this score, though the offence is far
graver when the same tendency appears, as it sometimes
does, in his letters to women. There is no proof that
Pope was ever licentious in practice. He was probably more
temperate than most of his companions, and could be accused
of fewer lapses from strict morality than, for example, the
excellent but thoughtless Steele. For this there was the
very good reason that his " little, tender, crazy carcass," as
Wycherley calls it, was utterly unfit for such excesses as
his companions could practise with comparative impunity.
He was bound under heavy penalties to be through life
a valetudinarian, and such doses of wine as the respectable
Addison used regularly to absorb, would have brought
speedy punishment. Pope's loose talk probably meant
little enough in the way of actual vice, though, as I have
already said, Trumbull saw reasons for friendly warning.
But some of his writings are stained by pruriency and
downright obscenity ; whilst the same fault may be connected with a painful absence of that chivalrous feeling
towards women which redeems Steele's errors of conduct
in our estimate of his character. Pope always takes a low,
sometimes a brutal view of the relation between the sexes.

Enough, however, has been said upon this point. If
Pope erred, he was certainly unfortunate in the objects of
his youthful hero-worship. Cromwell seems to have been
but a pedantic hanger-on of literary circles. His other

great friend, Wycherley, had stronger claims upon his
respect, but certainly was not likely to raise his standard
of delicacy.   Wycherley was a relic of a past literary
epoch.   He was nearly fifty years older than Pope.   His
last play, the *Plain Dealer*, had been produced in
1677, eleven years before Pope's birth.   The *Plain
Dealer* and the *Country Wife*, his chief performances,
are conspicuous amongst the comedies of the Restoration dramatists for sheer brutality.   During Pope's
boyhood he was an elderly rake about town, having
squandered his intellectual as well as his pecuniary
resources, but still scribbling bad verses and maxims on
the model of Rochefoucauld.   Pope had a very excusable, perhaps we may say creditable, enthusiasm for
the acknowledged representatives of literary glory.   Before
he was twelve years old he had persuaded some one to
take him to Will's, that he might have a sight of the vene-
rable Dryden ; and in the first published letter[1] to Wycherley he refers to this brief glimpse, and warmly thanks
Wycherley for some conversation about the elder poet.
And thus, when he came to know Wycherley, he was en-
raptured with the honour.   He followed the great man
about, as he tells us, like a dog ; and, doubtless, received with profound respect the anecdotes of literary life
which fell from the old gentleman's lips.   Soon a correspondence began, in which Pope adopts a less jaunty air
than that of his letters to Cromwell, but which is con-
ducted on both sides in the laboured complimentary style
which was not unnatural in the days when Congreve's
comedy was taken to represent the conversation of fashionable life.   Presently, however, the letters began to turn

[1] The letter is, unluckily, of doubtful authenticity ; but it represents Pope's probable sentiments.

upon an obviously dangerous topic.   Pope was only seventeen when it occurred to his friend to turn him to account
as a literary assistant.   The lad had already shown considerable powers of versification, and was soon employing
them in the revision of some of the numerous compositions which amused Wycherley's leisure.   It would have
required, one might have thought, less than Wycherley's
experience to foresee the natural end of such an alliance.
Pope, in fact, set to work with great vigour in his favourite
occupation of correcting.   He hacked and hewed right
and left; omitted, compressed, rearranged, and occasionally
inserted additions of his own devising.   Wycherley's
memory had been enfeebled by illness, and now played
him strange tricks.   He was in the habit of reading himself to sleep with Montaigne, Rochefoucauld, and Racine.
Next morning he would, with entire unconsciousness,
write down as his own the thoughts of his author, or
repeat almost word for word some previous composition
of his own.   To remove such repetitions thoroughly would
require a very free application of the knife, and Pope
would not be slow to discover that he was wasting talents
fit for original work in botching and tinkering a mass of
rubbish.

   Any man of ripe years would have predicted the obvious consequences ; and, according to the ordinary story,
those consequences followed.   Pope became more plain-
speaking, and at last almost insulting in his language.
Wycherley ended by demanding the return of his manuscripts, in a letter showing his annoyance under a
veil of civility ; and Pope sent them back with a smart
reply, recommending Wycherley to adopt a previous
suggestion and turn his poetry into maxims after the
manner of Rochefoucauld.   The " old scribbler," says

Johnson, " was angry to see his pages defaced, and felt
more pain from the criticism than content from the amend-
ment of his faults."   The story is told at length, and with
his usual brilliance, by Macaulay, and has hitherto passed
muster with all Pope's biographers ; and, indeed, it is so
natural a story, and is so far confirmed by other statements of Pope, that it seems a pity to spoil it.   And yet it
must be at least modified, for we have aleady reached one
of those perplexities which force a biographer of Pope to
be constantly looking to his footsteps.   So numerous are
the contradictions which surround almost every incident
of the poet's career, that one is constantly in danger of
stumbling into some pitfall, or bound to cross it in gingerly fashion on the stepping-stone of a cautious "perhaps."
The letters which are the authority for this story have
undergone a manipulation from Pope himself, under circumstances to be hereafter noticed ; and recent researches
have shown that a very false colouring has been put upon
this as upon other passages.   The nature of this strange
perversion is a curious illustration of Pope's absorbing
vanity.

Pope, in fact, was evidently ashamed of the attitude
which he had not unnaturally adopted to his correspondent.   The first man of letters of his day could not
bear to reveal the full degree in which he had fawned
upon the decayed dramatist, whose inferiority to himself
was now plainly recognized.   He altered the whole tone
of the correspondence by omission, and still worse by addi-
tion.   He did not publish a letter in which Wycherley
gently remonstrates with his young admirer for excessive
adulation ; he omitted from his own letters the phrase
which had provoked the remonstrance ; and, with more
daring falsification, he manufactured an imaginary letter

C

to Wycherley out of a letter really addressed to his friend
Caryll. In this letter Pope had himself addressed to
Caryll a remonstrance similar to that which he had
received from Wycherley. When published as a letter to
Wycherley, it gives the impression that Pope, at the
age of seventeen, was already rejecting excessive compliments addressed to him by his experienced friend. By
these audacious perversions of the truth, Pope is enabled
to heighten his youthful independence, and to represent
himself as already exhibiting a graceful superiority to the
reception or the offering of incense ; whilst he thus
precisely inverts the relation which really existed between
himself and his correspondent.

The letters, again, when read with a due attention to
dates, shows that Wycherley's proneness to take offence
has at least been exaggerated. Pope's services to Wycherley were rendered on two separate occasions. The
first set of poems were corrected during 1706 and 1707,
and Wycherley, in speaking of this revision, far from
showing symptoms of annoyance, speaks with gratitude of Pope's kindness, and returns the expressions of
goodwill which accompanied his criticisms. Both these
expressions, and Wycherley's acknowledgment of them,
were omitted in Pope's publication. More than two years
elapsed, when (in April, 1710) Wycherley submitted a
new set of manuscripts to Pope's unflinching severity ;
and it is from the letters which passed in regard to
this last batch that the general impression as to the nature
of the quarrel has been derived. But these letters, again,
have been mutilated, and so mutilated as to increase the
apparent tartness of the mutual retorts ; and it must
therefore remain doubtful how far the coolness which
ensued was really due to the cause assigned. Pope,

writing at the time to Cromwell, expresses his vexation at the difference, and professes himself unable to account for it, though he thinks that his corrections may have been the cause of the rupture. An alternative rumour,[2] it seems, accused Pope of having written some satirical verses upon his friend. To discover the rights and wrongs of the quarrel is now impossible, though, unfortunately, one thing is clear, namely, that Pope was guilty of grossly sacrificing truth in the interests of his own vanity. We may, indeed, assume, without much risk of error, that Pope had become too conscious of his own importance to find pleasure or pride in doctoring another man's verses. It must remain uncertain how far he showed this resentment to Wycherley openly, or gratified it by some covert means ; and how far, again, he succeeded in calming Wycherley's susceptibility by his compliments, or aroused his wrath by more or less contemptuous treatment of his verses.

A year after the quarrel, Cromwell reported that Wycherley had again been speaking in friendly terms of Pope, and Pope expressed his pleasure with eagerness. He must, he said, be more agreeable .to himself when agreeable to Wycherley, as the earth was brighter when the sun was less overcast. Wycherley, it may be remarked, took Pope's advice by turning some of his verses into prose maxims ; and they seem to have been at last upon more or less friendly terms. The final scene of Wycherley's questionable career, some four years later, is given by Pope in a letter to his friend, Edward Blount. The old man, he says, joined the sacraments of marriage and extreme unction. By one he supposed himself to gain some advantage of his soul ; by the other, he had the

[2] See Elwin's Pope, Vol. I., cxxxv.

pleasure of saddling his hated heir and nephew with the jointure of his widow. When dying, he begged his wife to grant him a last request, and, upon her consent, explained it to be that she would never again marry an old man. Sickness, says Pope in comment, often destroys wit and wisdom, but has seldom the power to remove humour. Wycherley's joke, replies a critic, is contemptible; and yet one feels that the death scene, with this strange mixture of cynicism, spite, and superstition, half redeemed by imperturbable good temper, would not be unworthy of a place in Wycherley's own school of comedy. One could wish that Pope had shown a little more perception of the tragic side of such a conclusion.

Pope was still almost a boy when he broke with Wycherley; but he was already beginning to attract attention, and within a surprisingly short time he was becoming known as one of the first writers of the day. I must now turn to the poems by which this reputation was gained, and the incidents connected with their publication. In Pope's life, almost more than in that of any other poet, the history of the author is the history of the man.

CHAPTER II.

POPE'S rupture with Wycherley took place in the summer of 1710, when Pope, therefore, was just twenty-two. He was at this time only known as the contributor of some small poems to a Miscellany. Three years afterwards (1713) he was receiving such patronage in his great undertaking, the translation of Homer, as to prove conclusively that he was regarded by the leaders of literature as a poet of very high promise; and two years later (1715) the appearance of the first volume of his translation entitled him to rank as the first poet of the day. So rapid a rise to fame has had few parallels, and was certainly not approached until Byron woke and found himself famous at twenty-four. Pope was eager for the praise of remarkable precocity, and was weak and insincere enough to alter the dates of some of his writings in order to strengthen his claim. Yet, even when we accept the corrected accounts of recent enquirers, there is no doubt that he gave proofs at a very early age of an extraordinary command of the resources of his art. It is still more evident that his merits were promptly and frankly recognized by his contemporaries. Great men and distinguished authors held out friendly hands to him; and he never had to undergo, even for a brief period, the dreary

ordeal of neglect through which men of loftier but less
popular genius, have been so often compelled to pass. And
yet it unfortunately happened that, even in this early
time, when success followed success, and the young man's
irritable nerves might well have been soothed by the
general chorus of admiration he excited and returned
bitter antipathies, some of which lasted through his life.

Pope's works belong to three distinct periods. The translation of Homer was the great work of the middle period
of his life. In his later years he wrote the moral and satirical poems by which he is now best known. The earlier
period, with which I have now to deal, was one of experi-
mental excursions into various fields of poetry, with varying
success and rather uncertain aim. Pope had already, as we
have seen, gone through the process of "filling his
basket." He had written the epic poem which happily
found its way into the flames. He had translated many
passages that struck his fancy in the classics, especially
considerable fragments of Ovid and Statius. Following
Dryden, he had turned some of Chaucer into modern
English; and, adopting a fashion which had not as yet
quite died of inanition, he had composed certain pastorals
in the manner of Theocritus and Virgil. These early productions had been written under the eye of Trumbull;
they had been handed about in manuscript; Wycherley,
as already noticed, had shown them to Walsh, himself an
offender of the same class. Granville, afterwards Lord
Lansdowne, another small poet, read them, and professed
to see in Pope another Virgil; whilst Congreve,
Garth, Somers, Halifax, and other men of weight, condescended to read, admire, and criticize. Old Tonson,
who had published for Dryden, wrote a polite note to
Pope, then only seventeen, saying that he had seen one of

the Pastorals in the hands of Congreve and Walsh, "which was extremely fine," and requesting the honour of printing it. Three years afterwards it accordingly appeared in Tonson's Miscellany, a kind of annual, of which the first numbers had been edited by Dryden. Such miscellanies more or less discharged the function of a modern magazine. The plan, said Pope to Wycherley, is very useful to the poets, "who, like other thieves, escape by getting into a crowd." The volume contained contributions from Buckingham, Garth, and Rowe; it closed with Pope's Pastorals, and opened with another set of pastorals by Ambrose Philips—a combination which, as we shall see, led to one of Pope's first quarrels.

The Pastorals have been seriously criticized; but they are, in truth, mere school-boy exercises; they represent nothing more than so many experiments in versification. The pastoral form had doubtless been used in earlier hands to embody true poetic feeling; but in Pope's time it had become hopelessly threadbare. The fine gentlemen in wigs and laced coats amused themselves by writing about nymphs and "conscious swains," by way of asserting their claims to elegance of taste. Pope, as a boy, took the matter seriously, and always retained a natural fondness for a juvenile performance upon which he had expended great labour, and which was the chief proof of his extreme precocity. He invites attention to his own merits, and claims especially the virtue of propriety. He does not, he tells us, like some other people, make his roses and daffodils bloom in the same season, and cause his nightingales to sing in November; and he takes particular credit for having remembered that there were no wolves in England, and having accordingly excised a passage in which Alexis prophesied that those animals would grow milder as they

listened to the strains of his favourite nymph. When a
man has got so far as to bring to England all the pagan
deities, and rival shepherds contending for bowls and lambs
in alternate strophes, these niceties seem a little out of
place. After swallowing such a camel of an anachronism
as is contained in the following lines, it is ridiculous to
pride oneself upon straining at a gnat :—

Inspire me, says Strephon,

> Inspire me, Phœbus, in my Delia's praise
> With Waller's strains or Granville's moving lays.
> A milkwhite bull shall at your altars stand,
> That threats a fight, and spurns the rising sand.

Granville would certainly not have felt more surprised
at meeting a wolf, than at seeing a milk-white bull sacrificed to Phœbus on the banks of the Thames. It would be
a more serious complaint that Pope, who can thus admit
anachronisms as daring as any of those which provoked
Johnson in Lycidas, shows none of that exquisite feeling
for rural scenery which is one of the superlative charms of
Milton's early poems. Though country-bred, he talks
about country sights and sounds as if he had been brought
up at Christ's Hospital, and read of them only in Virgil.
But, in truth, it is absurd to dwell upon such points. The
sole point worth notice in the Pastorals is the general
sweetness of the versification. Many corrections show how
carefully Pope had elaborated these early lines, and by
what patient toil he was acquiring the peculiar qualities of
style in which he was to become pre-eminent. We may
agree with Johnson that Pope performing upon a pastoral
pipe is rather a ludicrous person, but for mere practice
even nonsense verses have been found useful.

The young gentleman was soon to give a far more
characteristic specimen of his peculiar powers. Poets,

according to the ordinary rule, should begin by exuberant fancy, and learn to prune and refine as the reasoning faculties develope. But Pope was from the first a conscious and deliberate artist. He had read the fashionable critics of his time, and had accepted their canons as an embodiment of irrefragable reason. His head was full of maxims, some of which strike us as palpable truisms, and others as typical specimens of wooden pedantry. Dryden had set the example of looking upon the French critics as authoritative lawgivers in poetry. Boileau's art of poetry was carefully studied, as bits of it were judiciously appropriated by Pope. Another authority was the great Bossu, who wrote in 1675 a treatise on epic poetry ; and the modern reader may best judge of the doctrines characteristic of the school, by the naïve pedantry with which Addison, the typical man of taste of his time, invokes the authority of Bossu and Aristotle, in his exposition of Paradise Lost.[1] English writers were treading in the steps of Boileau and Horace. Roscommon selected for a poem the lively topic of "translated verse," and Sheffield had written with Dryden an essay upon satire, and afterwards a more elaborate essay upon poetry. To these masterpieces, said Addison, another masterpiece was now added by Pope's Essay upon Criticism. Not only did Addison applaud, but later critics have spoken of their wonder at the penetration, learning, and taste exhibited by so young a man. The essay was carefully finished. Written apparently in 1709, it was published in 1711. This was as short a time, said Pope to Spence, as he ever let anything of his lie by him ; he

---

Any poet who followed Bossu's rules, said Voltaire, might be certain that no one would read him ; happily it was impossible to follow them.

no doubt employed it, according to his custom, in correcting and revising, and he had prepared himself by carefully
digesting the whole in prose. It is, however, written
without any elaborate logical plan, though it is quite sufficiently coherent for its purpose. The maxims on which
Pope chiefly dwells are, for the most part, the obvious
rules which have been the common property of all gene-
rations of critics. One would scarcely ask for originality
in such a case, any more than one would desire a writer on
ethics to invent new laws of morality. We require neither
Pope nor Aristotle to tell us that critics should not be
pert nor prejudiced ; that fancy should be regulated by
judgment ; that apparent facility comes by long training ;
that the sound should have some conformity to the meaning ; that genius is often envied ; and that dulness is frequently beyond the reach of reproof. We might even
guess, without the authority of Pope, backed by Bacon,
that there are some beauties which cannot be taught by
method, but must be reached " by a kind of felicity." It
is not the less interesting to notice Pope's skill in polish-
ing these rather rusty sayings into the appearance of
novelty. In a familiar line Pope gives us the view which
he would himself apply in such cases.

> True wit is nature to advantage dress'd,
> What oft was thought, but ne'er so well express'd.

The only fair question, in short, is whether Pope has
managed to give a lasting form to some of the floating
commonplaces which have more or less suggested themselves to every writer. If we apply this test, we must
admit that if the essay upon criticism does not show deep
thought, it shows singular skill in putting old truths.
Pope undeniably succeeded in hitting off many phrases

of marked felicity. He already showed the power, in which he was probably unequalled, of coining aphorisms out of commonplace. Few people read the essay now, but everybody is aware that "fools rush in where angels fear to tread," and has heard the warning—

> A little learning is a dangerous thing,
> Drink deep, or taste not the Pierian spring—

maxims which may not commend themselves as strictly accurate to a scientific reasoner, but which have as much truth as one can demand from an epigram. And besides many sayings which share in some degree their merit, there are occasional passages which rise, at least, to the height of graceful rhetoric if they are scarcely to be called poetical. One simile was long famous, and was called by Johnson the best in the language. It is that in which the sanguine youth, overwhelmed by a growing perception of the boundlessness of possible attainments, is compared to the traveller crossing the mountains, and seeing—

> Hills peep o'er hills and Alps on Alps arise.

The poor simile is pretty well forgotten, but is really a good specimen of Pope's brilliant declamation.

The essay, however, is not uniformly polished. Between the happier passages we have to cross stretches of flat prose twisted into rhyme; Pope seems to have intentionally pitched his style at a prosaic level as fitter for didactic purposes; but besides this we here and there come upon phrases which are not only elliptical and slovenly, but defy all grammatical construction. This was a blemish to which Pope was always strangely liable. It was perhaps due in part to over-correction, when the context was forgotten and the subject had lost its fresh-

ness. Critics, again, have remarked upon the poverty of
the rhymes, and observed that he makes ten rhymes to
" wit " and twelve to " sense." The frequent recurrence
of the words is the more awkward because they are
curiously ambiguous. " Wit " was beginning to receive
its modern meaning ; but Pope uses it vaguely as sometimes equivalent to intelligence in general, sometimes
to the poetic faculty, and sometimes to the erratic
fancy, which the true poet restrains by sense. Pope
would have been still more puzzled if asked to define
precisely what he meant by the antithesis between nature
and art. They are somehow opposed, yet art turns out
to be only " nature methodized." We have indeed a clue
for our guidance ; to study nature, we are told, is the
same thing as to study Homer, and Homer should be
read day and night, with Virgil for a comment and
Aristotle for an expositor. Nature, good sense, Homer,
Virgil, and the Stagyrite all, it seems, come to much the
same thing.

It would be very easy to pick holes in this very loose
theory. But it is better to try to understand the point
of view indicated ; for, in truth, Pope is really stating the
assumptions which guided his whole career. No one will
accept his position at the present time ; but any one who
is incapable of, at least, a provisional sympathy, may as
well throw Pope aside at once, and with Pope most contemporary literature.

The dominant figure in Pope's day was the Wit.
The wit—taken personally—was the man who represented what we now describe by culture or the spirit of
the age. Bright clear common sense was for once having
its own way, and tyrannizing over the faculties from which
it too often suffers violence. The favoured faculty

never doubted its own qualification for supremacy in every department. In metaphysics it was triumphing with Hobbes and Locke over the remnants of scholasticism; under Tillotson, it was expelling mystery from religion; and in art it was declaring war against the extravagant, the romantic, the mystic, and the Gothic,—a word then used as a simple term of abuse. Wit and sense are but different avatars of the same spirit; wit was the form in which it showed itself in coffee-houses, and sense that in which it appeared in the pulpit or parliament. When Walsh told Pope to be correct, he was virtually advising him to carry the same spirit into poetry. The classicism of the time was the natural corollary; for the classical models were the historical symbols of the movement which Pope represented. He states his view very tersely in the essay. Classical culture had been overwhelmed by the barbarians, and the monks "finished what the Goths began." Letters revived when the study of classical models again gave an impulse and supplied a guidance.

> At length Erasmus, that great injured name,
> The glory of the priesthood and their shame,
> Stemm'd the wild torrent of a barbarous age,
> And drove these holy Vandals off the stage.

The classicalism of Pope's time was no doubt very different from that of the period of Erasmus; but in his view it differed only because the contemporaries of Dryden had more thoroughly dispersed the mists of the barbarism which still obscured the Shaksperean age, and from which even Milton or Cowley had not completely escaped. Dryden and Boileau and the French critics, with their interpreters Roscommon, Sheffield, and Walsh, who found rules in Aristotle, and drew their

precedents from Homer, were at last stating the pure
canons of unadulterated sense. To this school, wit and
sense, and nature, and the classics, all meant pretty much
the same. That was pronounced to be unnatural which
was too silly, or too far-fetched, or too exalted, to approve
itself to the good sense of a wit ; and the very incarnation
and eternal type of good sense and nature was to be
found in the classics. The test of thorough polish and
refinement was the power of ornamenting a speech with an
appropriate phrase from Horace or Virgil, or prefixing a
Greek motto to an essay in the *Spectator*. If it was
necessary to give to any utterance an air of philosophical
authority, a reference to Longinus or Aristotle was the
natural device. Perhaps the acquaintance with classics
might not be very profound ; but the classics supplied
at least a convenient symbol for the spirit which had
triumphed against Gothic barbarism and scholastic
pedantry.

Even the priggish wits of that day were capable of
being bored by didactic poetry, and especially by such
didactic poetry as resolved itself too easily into a string
of maxims, not more poetical in substance than the immortal " 'Tis a sin to steal a pin." The essay—published
anonymously — did not make any rapid success till
Pope sent round copies to well-known critics. Addison's
praise and Dennis's abuse helped, as we shall presently
see, to give it notoriety. Pope, however, returned from
criticism to poetry, and his next performance was in
some degree a fresh, but far less puerile, performance upon
the pastoral pipe.[2] Nothing could be more natural than

---

[2] There is the usual contradiction as to the date of composition
of *WindsorForest*. Part seems to have been written early (Pope
says 1704), and part certainly not before 1712.

for the young poet to take for a text the forest in which
he lived. Dull as the natives might be, their dwelling-
place was historical, and there was an excellent precedent
for such a performance. Pope, as we have seen, was
familiar with Milton's juvenile poems ; but such works as
the Allegro and Penseroso were too full of the genuine
country spirit to suit his probable audience. Wycherley,
whom he frequently invited to come to Binfield, would
undoubtedly have found Milton a bore. But Sir John
Denham, a thoroughly masculine, if not, as Pope calls
him, a majestic poet, was a guide whom the Wycherleys
would respect. His *Cooper's Hill* (in 1642) was the first
example of what Johnson calls local poetry—poetry, that
is, devoted to the celebration of a particular place ; and,
moreover, it was one of the early models of the rhythm
which became triumphant in the hands of Dryden. One
couplet is still familiar :—

> Though deep, yet clear ; though gentle, yet not dull ;
> Strong without rage ; without o'erflowing, full.

The poem has some vigorous descriptive touches, but is
in the main a forcible expression of the moral and political reflections which would be approved by the admirers
of good sense in poetry.

Pope's *Windsor Forest*, which appeared in the beginning of 1713, is closely and avowedly modelled upon
this original. There is still a considerable infusion of
the puerile classicism of the Pastorals, which contrasts
awkwardly with Denham's strength, and a silly episode
about the nymph Lodona changed into the river Loddon
by Diana, to save her from the pursuit of Pan. But the
style is animated, and the descriptions, though seldom
original, show Pope's frequent felicity of language.

Wordsworth, indeed, was pleased to say that Pope had
here introduced almost the only "new images of internal
nature" to be found between Milton and Thomson.
Probably the good Wordsworth was wishing to do a little
bit of excessive candour.   Pope will not introduce his
scenery without a turn suited to the taste of the town:—

> Here waving groves a chequer'd scene display,
> And part admit and part exclude the day ;
> As some coy nymph her lover's fond address,
> Nor quite indulges nor can quite repress.

He has some well turned lines upon the sports of the
forest, though they are clearly not the lines of a sports-
man.   They betray something of the sensitive lad's
shrinking from the rough squires whose only literature
consisted of Durfey's songs, and who would have heartily
laughed at his sympathy for a dying pheasant.   I may
observe in passing that Pope always showed the true
poet's tenderness for the lower animals, and disgust at
bloodshed.   He loved his dog, and said that he would
have inscribed over his grave, " O rare Bounce," but for
the appearance of ridiculing " rare Ben Jonson."   He
spoke with horror of a contemporary dissector of live
dogs, and the pleasantest of his papers in the *Guardian*
is a warm remonstrance against cruelty to animals.   He
" dares not " attack hunting, he says—and, indeed, such
an attack requires some courage even at the present day—
but he evidently has no sympathy with huntsmen, and
has to borrow his description from Statius, which was
hardly the way to get the true local colour.   *Windsor
Forest*, however, like *Cooper's Hill*, speedily diverges into
historical and political reflections.   The barbarity of the
old forest laws, the poets Denham and Cowley and
Surrey, who had sung on the banks of the Thames, and

the heroes who made Windsor illustrious, suggest obvious thoughts, put into verses often brilliant, though sometimes affected, varied by a compliment to Trumbull and an excessive eulogy of Granville, to whom the poem is inscribed. The whole is skilfully adapted to the time by a brilliant eulogy upon the peace which was concluded just as the poem was published. The Whig poet Tickell, soon to be Pope's rival, was celebrating the same " lofty theme " on his " artless reed," and introducing a pretty little compliment to Pope. To readers who have lost the taste for poetry of this class one poem may seem about as good as the other ; but Pope's superiority is plain enough to a reader who will condescend to distinguish. His verses are an excellent specimen of his declamatory style— polished, epigrammatic, and well expressed ; and, though keeping far below the regions of true poetry, preserving just that level which would commend them to the literary statesmen and the politicians at Will's and Button's. Perhaps some advocate of Free Trade might try upon a modern audience the lines in which Pope expresses his aspiration in a footnote that London may one day become a " FREE PORT." There is at least not one antiquated or obscure phrase in the whole. Here are half-a-dozen lines :—

> The time shall come, when, free as seas and wind,
> Unbounded Thames shall flow for all mankind,
> Whole nations enter with each swelling tide,
> And seas but join the regions they divide ;
> Earth's distant ends our glory shall behold,
> And the new world launch forth to seek the old.

In the next few years Pope found other themes for the display of his declamatory powers. Of the *Temple of Fame* (1715), a frigid imitation of Chaucer, I need only say that it is one of Pope's least successful performances ;

D

but I must notice more fully two rhetorical poems which appeared in 1717. These were the *Elegy to the Memory of
an Unfortunate Lady* and the *Eloisa to Abelard*. Both
poems, and especially the last, have received the warmest
praises from Pope's critics, and even from critics who
were most opposed to his school. They are, in fact, his
chief performances of the sentimental kind. Written in
his youth, and yet when his powers of versification had
reached their fullest maturity, they represent an element
generally absent from his poetry. Pope was at the period
in which, if ever, a poet should sing of love, and in which
we expect the richest glow and fervour of youthful imagination. Pope was neither a Burns, nor a Byron, nor a
Keats ; but here, if anywhere, we should find those
qualities in which he has most affinity to the poets of
passion or of sensuous emotion, not soured by experience
or purified by reflection. The motives of the two poems
were skilfully chosen. Pope—as has already appeared to
some extent—was rarely original in his designs ; he liked to
have the outlines at last drawn for him, to be filled with
his own colouring. The *Eloisa to Abelard* was founded
upon a translation from the French, published in 1714 by
Hughes (author of the *Siege of Damascus*), which is itself
a manipulated translation from the famous Latin originals.
Pope, it appears, kept very closely to the words of the
English translation, and in some places has done little
more than versify the prose, though, of course, it is compressed, rearranged, and modified. The *Unfortunate
Lady* has been the cause of a good deal of controversy.
Pope's elegy implies, vaguely enough, that she had been
cruelly treated by her guardians, and had committed
suicide in some foreign country. The verses, as commentators decided, showed such genuine feeling, that

the story narrated in them must have been authentic, and one of his own correspondents (Caryll) begged him for an explanation of the facts. Pope gave no answer, but left a posthumous note to an edition of his letters calculated, perhaps intended, to mystify future inquirers. The lady, a Mrs. Weston, to whom the note pointed, did not die till 1724, and could therefore not have committed suicide in 1717. The mystification was childish enough, though if Pope had committed no worse crime of the kind, one would not consider him to be a very grievous offender. The inquiries of Mr. Dilke, who cleared up this puzzle, show that there were in fact two ladies, Mrs. Weston and a Mrs. Cope, known to Pope about this time, both of whom suffered under some domestic persecution. Pope seems to have taken up their cause with energy, and sent money to Mrs. Cope when, at a later period, she was dying abroad in great distress. His zeal seems to have been sincere and generous, and it is possible enough that the elegy was a reflection of his feelings, though it suggested an imaginary state of facts. If this be so, the reference to the lady in his posthumous note contained some relation to the truth, though if taken too literally it would be misleading.

The poems themselves are, beyond all doubt, impressive compositions. They are vivid and admirably worked. " Here," says Johnson of the *Eloisa to Abelard*, the most important of the two, " is particularly observable the *curiosa felicitas*, a fruitful soil and careful cultivation. Here is no crudeness of sense, nor asperity of language." So far there can be no dispute. The style has the highest degree of technical perfection, and it is generally added that the poems are as pathetic as they are exquisitely written. Bowles, no hearty lover of Pope, declared the

Eloisa to be "infinitely superior to everything of the
kind, ancient or modern." The tears shed, says Hazlitt
of the same poem, "are drops gushing from the heart;
the words are burning sighs breathed from the soul of
love." And De Quincey ends an eloquent criticism by
declaring that the "lyrical tumult of the changes, the
hope, the tears, the rapture, the penitence, the despair,
place the reader in tumultuous sympathy with the poor
distracted nun." The pathos of the *Unfortunate Lady*
has been almost equally praised, and I may quote from it
a famous passage which Mackintosh repeated with emotion
to repel a charge of coldness brought against Pope :—

> By foreign hands thy dying eyes were closed,
> By foreign hands thy decent limbs composed,
> By foreign hands thy humble grave adorn'd,
> By strangers honour'd and by strangers mourn'd !
> What though no friends in sable weeds appear,
> Grieve for an hour, perhaps, then mourn a year,
> And bear about the mockery of woe
> To midnight dances and the public show ?
> What though no weeping loves thy ashes grace,
> Nor polish'd marble emulate thy face ?
> What though no sacred earth allow thee room,
> Nor hallow'd dirge be mutter'd o'er thy tomb ?
> Yet shall thy grave with rising flowers be dress'd,
> And the green turf lie lightly on thy breast ;
> There shall the morn her earliest tears bestow,
> There the first roses of the year shall blow ;
> While angels with their silver wings o'ershade
> The ground, now sacred by thy reliques made.

The more elaborate poetry of the *Eloisa* is equally polished
throughout, and too much praise cannot easily be bestowed
upon the skill with which the romantic scenery of the
convent is indicated in the background, and the force
with which Pope has given the revulsions of feeling of

his unfortunate heroine from earthly to heavenly love, and from keen remorse to renewed gusts of overpowering passion. All this may be said, and without opposing high critical authority. And yet, I must also say, whether with or without authority, that I, at least, can read the poems without the least " disposition to cry," and that a single pathetic touch of Cowper or Wordsworth strikes incomparably deeper. And if I seek for a reason, it seems to be simply that Pope never crosses the undefinable, but yet ineffaceable, line which separates true poetry from rhetoric. The Eloisa ends rather flatly by one of Pope's characteristic aphorisms. " He best can paint them (the woes, that is, of Eloisa) who shall feel them most ; " and it is characteristic, by the way, that even in these his most impassioned verses, the lines which one remembers are of the same epigrammatic stamp, e.g. :

> A heap of dust alone remains of thee,
> 'Tis all thou art and all the proud shall be !

> I mourn the lover, not lament the fault.

> How happy is the blameless vestal's lot,
> The world forgetting, by the world forgot.

The worker in moral aphorisms cannot forget himself even in the full swing of his fervid declamation. I have no doubt that Pope so far exemplified his own doctrine that he truly felt whilst he was writing. His feelings make him eloquent, but they do not enable him to " snatch a grace beyond the reach of art," to blind us for a moment to the presence of the consummate workman, judiciously blending his colours, heightening his effects, and skilfully managing his transitions or consciously introducing an abrupt outburst of a new mood. The smoothness of the verses imposes monotony even upon the varying pas- ·

sions which are supposed to struggle in Eloisa's breast. It is not merely our knowledge that Pope is speaking dramatically which prevents us from receiving the same kind of impressions as we receive from poetry—such, for example, as some of Cowper's minor pieces—into which we know that a man is really putting his whole heart. The comparison would not be fair, for in such cases we are moved by knowledge of external facts as well as by the poetic power. But it is simply that Pope always resembles an orator whose gestures are studied, and who thinks while he is speaking of the fall of his robes and the attitude of his hands. He is throughout academical; and though knowing with admirable nicety how grief should be represented, and what have been the expedients of his best predecessors, he misses the one essential touch of spontaneous impulse.

One other blemish is perhaps more fatal to the popularity of the Eloisa. There is a taint of something unwholesome and effeminate. Pope, it is true, is only following the language of the original in the most offensive passages; but we see too plainly that he has dwelt too fondly upon those passages, and worked them up with especial care. We need not be prudish in our judgment of impassioned poetry; but when the passion has this false ring, the ethical coincides with the æsthetic objection.

I have mentioned these poems here, because they seem to be the development of the rhetorical vein which appeared in the earlier work. But I have passed over another work which has sometimes been regarded as his masterpiece. A Lord Petre had offended a Miss Fermor by stealing a lock of her hair. She thought that he showed more gallantry than courtesy, and some unpleasant feeling resulted between the families. Pope's friend, Caryll, thought that it might be appeased if the young poet would turn the whole affair into friendly ridicule. Nobody, it might well be supposed, had a more dexterous touch ; and a brilliant trifle from his hands, just fitted for the atmosphere of drawing-rooms, would be a convenient peace-offering, and was the very thing in which he might be expected to succeed. Pope accordingly set to work at a dainty little mock-heroic, in which he describes, in playful mockery of the conventional style, the fatal coffee-drinking at Hampton, in which the too daring peer appropriated the lock. The poem received the praise which it well deserved ; for certainly the young poet had executed his task to a nicety. No more brilliant, sparkling, vivacious trifle, is to be found in our literature than the *Rape of the Lock*, even in this early form. Pope received permission from the lady to publish it in Lintot's Miscellany in 1712, and a wider circle admired it, though it seems that the lady and her family began to think that young Mr. Pope was making rather too free with her name. Pope meanwhile, animated by his success, hit upon a singularly happy conception, by which he thought that the poem might be rendered more important. The solid critics of those days were much occupied with the machinery of epic poems ; the machinery being composed of the gods and goddesses who, from the days of Homer, had attended to the fortunes of heroes. He had hit upon a curious French book, the *Comte de Gabalis*, which professes to reveal the mysteries of the Rosicrucians, and it occurred to him that the elemental sylphs and gnomes would serve his purpose admirably. He spoke of his new device to Addison, who administered— and there is not the slightest reason for doubting his per-

fect sincerity and good meaning—a little dose of cold
water.   The poem, as it stood, was a "delicious little
thing"—*merum sal*—and it would be a pity to alter it.
Pope, however, adhered to his plan, made a splendid
success, and thought that Addison must have been
prompted by some mean motive.   The *Rape of the Lock*
appeared in its new form, with sylphs and gnomes, and
an ingenious account of a game at cards and other im-
provements, in 1714.   Pope declared, and critics have
agreed, that he never showed more skill than in the
remodelling of this poem ; and it has ever since held a
kind of recognised supremacy amongst the productions of
the drawing-room muse.

The reader must remember that the so-called heroic
style of Pope's period is now hopelessly effete.   No human
being would care about machinery and the rules of Bossu,
or read without utter weariness the mechanical imitations
of Homer and Virgil which were occasionally attempted
by the Blackmores and other less ponderous versifiers.
The shadow grows dim with the substance.   The burlesque loses its point when we care nothing for the original ; and, so far, Pope's bit of filigree-work, as Hazlitt
calls it, has become tarnished.   The very mention of
beaux and belles suggests the kind of feeling with which
we disinter fragments of old-world finery from the depths
of an ancient cabinet, and even the wit is apt to sound
wearisome.   And further, it must be allowed to some
hostile critics that Pope has a worse defect.   The poem
is, in effect, a satire upon feminine frivolity.   It continues
the strain of mockery against hoops and patches and their
wearers, which supplied Addison and his colleagues with
the materials of so many *Spectators*.   I think that even
in Addison there is something which rather jars upon us.

His persiflage is full of humour and kindliness, but underlying it there is a tone of superiority to women which is sometimes offensive. It is taken for granted that a woman is a fool, or at least should be flattered if any man condescends to talk sense to her. With Pope this tone becomes harsher, and the merciless satirist begins to show himself. In truth, Pope can be inimitably pungent, but he can never be simply playful. Addison was too condescending with his pretty pupils; but under Pope's courtesy there lurks contempt, and his smile has a disagreeable likeness to a sneer. If Addison's manner sometimes suggests the blandness of a don who classes women with the inferior beings unworthy of the Latin grammar, Pope suggests the brilliant wit whose contempt has a keener edge from his resentment against fine ladies blinded to his genius by his personal deformity.

Even in his dedication, Pope, with unconscious impertinence, insults his heroine for her presumable ignorance of his critical jargon. His smart epigrams want but a slight change of tone to become satire. It is the same writer who begins an essay on women's characters by telling a woman that her sex is a compound of

> Matter too soft a lasting mask to bear;
> And best distinguished by black, brown, or fair,

and communicates to her the pleasant truth that

> Every woman is at heart a rake.

Women, in short, are all frivolous beings, whose one genuine interest is in love-making. The same sentiment is really implied in the more playful lines in the *Rape of the Lock*. The sylphs are warned by omens that some misfortune impends; but they don't know what.

> Whether the nymph shall break Diana's law,
> Or some frail china jar receive a flaw;

> Or stain her honour or her new brocade,
> Forget her prayers or miss a masquerade;
> Or lose her heart or necklace at a ball,
> Or whether heaven has doom'd that Shock must fall.

We can understand that Miss Fermor would feel such
raillery to be equivocal. It may be added, that an equal
want of delicacy is implied in the mock-heroic battle at
the end, where the ladies are gifted with an excess of
screaming power :—

> ' Restore the lock ! ' she cries, and all around
> ' Restore the lock,' the vaulted roofs rebound—
> Not fierce Othello in so loud a strain
> Roar'd for the handkerchief that caused his pain.

These faults, though far from trifling, are yet felt only
as blemishes in the admirable beauty and brilliance of
the poem. The successive scenes are given with so firm
and clear a touch—there is such a sense of form, the
language is such a dexterous elevation of the ordinary
social twaddle into the mock-heroic, that it is impossible not
to recognize a consummate artistic power. The dazzling
display of true wit and fancy blinds us for the time
to the want of that real tenderness and humour, which
would have softened some harsh passages, and given a
more enduring charm to the poetry. It has, in short, the
merit that belongs to any work of art which expresses
in the most finished form the sentiment characteristic of a
given social phase ; one deficient in many of the most
ennobling influences, but yet one in which the arts of con-
verse represent a very high development of shrewd sense
refined into vivid wit. And we may, I think, admit that
there is some foundation for the genealogy that traces
Pope's Ariel back to his more elevated ancestor in the
Tempest. The later Ariel, indeed, is regarded as the soul

of a coquette, and is almost an allegory of the spirit of
poetic fancy in slavery to polished society.

> Gums and pomatums shall his flight restrain
> While clogg'd he beats his silken wings in vain.

Pope's Ariel is a parody of the ethereal being into whom
Shakspeare had refined the ancient fairy ; but it is a parody
which still preserves a sense of the delicate and graceful.   The ancient race which appeared for the last time in
this travesty of the fashion of Queen Anne, still showed
some touch of its ancient beauty.   Since that time no
fairy has appeared without being hopelessly childish or
affected.

Let us now turn from the poems to the author's personal career during the same period.   In the remarkable
autobiographic poem called the *Epistle to Arbuthnot,*
Pope speaks of his early patrons and friends, and adds—

> Soft were my numbers; who could take offence
> When pure description held the place of sense ?
> Like gentle Fanny's was my flow'ry theme,
> A painted mistress or a purling stream.
> Yet then did Gildon draw his venal quill—
> I wish'd the man a dinner, and sat still.
> Yet then did Dennis rave in furious fret ;
> I never answer'd,—I was not in debt.

Pope's view of his own career suggests the curious problem : how it came to pass that so harmless a man should
be the butt of so many hostilities ?   How could any man
be angry with a writer of gentle pastorals and versified love-
letters ?   The answer of Pope was, that this was the normal
state of things.   "The life of a wit," he says, in the preface
to his works, "is a warfare upon earth ;" and the warfare
results from the hatred of men of genius natural to the dull.
Had any one else made such a statement, Pope would have

seen its resemblance to the complaint of the one reasonable
juryman overpowered by eleven obstinate fellows. But we
may admit that an intensely sensitive nature is a bad qualification for a public career. A man who ventures into
the throng of competitors without a skin will be tortured by every touch, and suffer the more if he turns to
retaliate.

Pope's first literary performances had not been so harmless as he suggests. Amongst the minor men of letters of
the day was the surly John Dennis. He was some thirty
years Pope's senior; a writer of dreary tragedies which
had gained a certain success by their Whiggish tendencies,
and of ponderous disquisitions upon critical questions,
not much cruder in substance though heavier in form than
many utterances of Addison or Steele. He could, however,
snarl out some shrewd things when provoked, and was
known to the most famous wits of the day. He had corresponded with Dryden, Congreve, and Wycherley, and published some of their letters. Pope, it seems, had been introduced to him by Cromwell, but they had met only two or
three times. When Pope had become ashamed of following Wycherley about like a dog, he would soon find out
that a Dennis did not deserve the homage of a rising
genius. Possibly Dennis had said something of Pope's
Pastorals, and Pope had probably been a witness, perhaps
more than a mere witness, to some passage of arms in
which Dennis lost his temper. In mere youthful impertinence he introduced an offensive touch in the *Essay upon
Criticism*. It would be well, he said, if critics could
advise authors freely,—

> But Appius reddens at each word you speak,
> And stares, tremendous, with a threatening eye,
> Like some fierce tyrant in old tapestry.

The name Appius referred to Dennis's tragedy of *Appius and Virginia,* a piece now recollected solely by the fact that poor Dennis had invented some new thunder for the performance; and by his piteous complaint against the actors for afterwards "stealing his thunder," had started a proverbial expression. Pope's reference stung Dennis to the quick. He replied by a savage pamphlet, pulling Pope's essay to pieces, and hitting some real blots, but diverging into the coarsest personal abuse. Not content with saying in his preface that he was attacked with the utmost false-hood and calumny by a little affected hypocrite, who had nothing in his mouth but truth, candour, and good-nature, he reviled Pope for his personal defects; insinu-ated that he was a hunch-backed toad; declared that he was the very shape of the bow of the god of love; that he might be thankful that he was born a modern, for had he been born of Greek parents his life would have been no longer than that of one of his poems, namely, half a day; and that his outward form, however like a monkey's, could not deviate more from the average of humanity than his mind. These amenities gave Pope his first taste of good savage slashing abuse. The revenge was out of all proportion to the offence. Pope, at first, seemed to take the assault judiciously. He kept silence, and simply marked some of the faults exposed by Dennis for alteration. But the wound rankled, and when an opportunity presently offered itself, Pope struck savagely at his enemy. To show how this came to pass, I must rise from poor old Dennis to a more exalted literary sphere.

The literary world, in which Dryden had recently been, and Pope was soon to be, the most conspicuous figure, was for the present under the mild dictatorship of

Addison.   We know Addison as one of the most kindly
and delicate of humourists, and we can perceive the
gentleness which made him one of the most charming of
companions in a small society.   His sense of the ludicrous
saved him from the disagreeable ostentation of powers
which were never applied to express bitterness of feeling or
to edge angry satire.   The reserve of his sensitive nature
made access difficult, but he was so transparently modest
and unassuming that his shyness was not, as is too often
the case, mistaken for pride.   It is easy to understand the
posthumous affection which Macaulay has so eloquently
expressed, and the contemporary popularity which, according to Swift, would have made people unwilling to refuse
him had he asked to be king.   And yet I think that one
cannot read Addison's praises without a certain recalcitra-
tion, like that which one feels in the case of the model boy
who wins all the prizes, including that for good conduct.
It is hard to feel very enthusiastic about a virtue whose
dictates coincide so precisely with the demands of decorum,
and which leads by so easy a path to reputation and success.
Popularity is more often significant of the tact which
makes a man avoid giving offence, than of the warm
impulses of a generous nature.   A good man who mixes
with the world ought to be hated, if not to hate.   But
whatever we may say against his excessive goodness,
Addison deserved and received universal esteem, which
in some cases became enthusiastic.   Foremost amongst
his admirers was the warm-hearted, reckless, impetuous
Steele, the typical Irishman ; and amongst other members
of his little senate—as Pope called it—were Ambrose
Philips and Tickell, young men of letters and sound
Whig politics, and more or less competitors of Pope in
literature.   When Pope was first becoming known in

London the Whigs were out of power; Addison and his friends were generally to be found at Button's Coffee-house in the afternoon, and were represented to the society of the time by the *Spectator*, which began in March, 1711, and appeared daily to the end of 1712. Naturally, the young Pope would be anxious to approach this famous clique, though his connexions lay in the first instance amongst the Jacobite and Catholic families. Steele, too, would be glad to welcome so promising a contributor to the *Spectator* and its successor the *Guardian*.

Pope, we may therefore believe, was heartily delighted when, some months after Dennis's attack, a notice of his *Essay upon Criticism* appeared in the *Spectator*, December 20, 1711. The reviewer censured some attacks upon contemporaries—a reference obviously to the lines upon Dennis—which the author had admitted into his " very fine poem ;" but there were compliments enough to overbalance this slight reproof. Pope wrote a letter of acknowledgment to Steele, overflowing with the sincerest gratitude of a young poet on his first recognition by a high authority. Steele, in reply, disclaimed the article, and promised to introduce Pope to its real author, the great Addison himself. It does not seem that the acquaintance thus opened with the Addisonians ripened very rapidly, or led to any considerable results. Pope, indeed, is said to have written some *Spectators*. He certainly sent to Steele his *Messiah*, a sacred eclogue in imitation of Virgil's *Pollio*. It appeared on May 14th, 1712, and is one of Pope's dexterous pieces of workmanship, in which phrases from Isaiah are so strung together as to form a good imitation of the famous poem which was once supposed to entitle Virgil to some place among the inspired heralds of Christianity. Pope sent

another letter or two to Steele, which look very much like
intended contributions to the *Spectator*, and a short letter
about Hadrian's verses to his soul, which appeared in November, 1712.   When, in 1713, the *Guardian* succeeded
the *Spectator*, Pope was one of Steele's contributors, and a
paper by him upon dedications appeared as the fourth
number.   He soon gave a more remarkable proof of his
friendly relations with Addison.

It is probable that no first performance of a play upon
the English stage ever excited so much interest as that of
Addison's *Cato*.   It was not only the work of the first
man of letters of the day, but it had, or was taken to
have, a certain political significance.   " The time was
come," says Johnson, "when those who affected to think
liberty in danger affected likewise to think that a stage-
play might preserve it."   Addison, after exhibiting more
than the usual display of reluctance, prepared his play
for representation, and it was undoubtedly taken to be in
some sense a Whig manifesto.   It was therefore remarkable that he should have applied to Pope for a prologue,
though Pope's connexions were entirely of the anti-
Whiggish kind, and a passage in *Windsor Forest*, his last
new poem (it appeared in March 1713), indicated pretty
plainly a refusal to accept the Whig shibboleths.   In
the *Forest* he was enthusiastic for the peace, and sneered
at the Revolution.   Pope afterwards declared that Addison had disavowed all party intentions at the time,
and he accused him of insincerity for afterwards taking
credit (in a poetical dedication of *Cato*) for the services
rendered by his play to the cause of liberty.   Pope's
assertion is worthless in any case where he could exalt his
own character for consistency at another man's expense,
but it is true that both parties were inclined to equivocate.

It is, indeed, difficult to understand how, if any " stage-play could preserve liberty," such a play as *Cato* should do the work. The polished declamation is made up of the platitudes common to Whigs and Tories ; and Boling-broke gave the cue to his own party when he presented fifty guineas to *Cato*'s representative for defending the cause of liberty so well against a perpetual dictator. The Whigs, said Pope, design a second present when they can contrive as good a saying. Bolingbroke was, of course, aiming at Marlborough, and his interpretation was intrinsically as plausible as any that could have been devised by his antagonists. Each side could adopt *Cato* as easily as rival sects can quote the Bible ; and it seems possible that Addison may have suggested to Pope that nothing in *Cato* could really offend his principles. Addison, as Pope also tells us, thought the prologue ambiguous, and altered "Britons, *arise !*" to "Britons, *attend !*" lest the phrase should be thought to hint at a new revolution. Addison advised Pope about this time not to be content with the applause of " half the nation," and perhaps regarded him as one who, by the fact of his external position with regard to parties, would be a more appropriate sponsor for the play.

Whatever the intrinsic significance of *Cato*, circum-stances gave it a political colour ; and Pope, in a lively description of the first triumphant night to his friend Caryll, says, that as author of the successful and very spirited prologue, he was clapped into a Whig, sorely against his will, at every two lines. Shortly before he had spoken in the warmest terms to the same correspondent of the admi-rable moral tendency of the work ; and perhaps he had not realized the full party significance till he became con-scious of the impression produced upon the audience. Not

E

long afterwards (letter of June 12, 1713), we find him
complaining that his connexion with Steele and the
Guardian was giving offence to some honest Jacobites.
Had they known the nature of the connexion, they need
hardly have grudged Steele his contributor. His next
proceedings possibly suggested the piece of advice which
Addison gave to Lady M. W. Montague : " Leave Pope
as soon as you can ; he will certainly play you some
devilish trick else."

His first trick was calculated to vex an editor's soul.
Ambrose Philips, as I have said, had published certain
pastorals in the same volume with Pope's. Philips, though
he seems to have been less rewarded than most of his companions, was certainly accepted as an attached member of
Addison's " little senate ;" and that body was not more
free than other mutual admiration societies from the desire
to impose its own prejudices upon the public. When
Philips's *Distressed Mother*, a close imitation of Racine's
Andromaque, was preparing for the stage, the Spectator
was taken by Will Honeycomb to a rehearsal (*Spectator*,
January 31, 1712), and Sir Roger de Coverley himself
attended one of the performances (*Ib.*, March, 25) and was
profoundly affected by its pathos. The last paper was of
course by Addison, and is a real triumph of art as a most
delicate application of humour to the slightly unworthy
purpose of puffing a friend and disciple. Addison had
again praised Philips's Pastorals in the *Spectator* (October
30, 1712), and amongst the early numbers of the *Guardian*
were a short series of papers upon pastoral poetry, in
which the fortunate Ambrose was again held up as a
model, whilst no notice was taken of Pope's rival performance. Pope, one may believe, had a contempt for Philips,
whose pastoral inanities, whether better or worse than his

own, had not the excuse of being youthful productions. Philips has bequeathed to our language the phrase " Namby-pamby," imposed upon him by Henry Carey (author of *Sally in our Alley*, and the clever farce *Chrononhotonthologos*), and years after this he wrote a poem to Miss Pulteney in the nursery, beginning,—

> "Dimply damsel, sweetly smiling,"

which may sufficiently interpret the meaning of his nickname. Pope's irritable vanity was vexed at the liberal praises bestowed on such a rival, and he revenged himself by an artifice more ingenious than scrupulous. He sent an anonymous article to Steele for the *Guardian*. It is a professed continuation of the previous papers on pastorals, and is ostensibly intended to remove the appearance of partiality arising from the omission of Pope's name. In the first paragraphs the design is sufficiently concealed to mislead an unwary reader into the belief that Philips is preferred to Pope ; but the irony soon becomes transparent, and Philips's antiquated affectation is contrasted with the polish of Pope, who is said even to " deviate into downright poetry." Steele, it is said, was so far mystified as to ask Pope's permission to publish the criticism. Pope generously permitted, and accordingly Steele printed what he must soon have discovered to be a shrewd attack upon his old friend and ally. Some writers have found a difficulty in understanding how Steele could have so blundered. One might, perhaps, whisper in confidence to the discreet, that even editors are mortal, and that Steele was conceivably capable of the enormity of reading papers carelessly. Philips was furious, and hung up a birch in Button's Coffee-house, declaring that he would apply it to his tormentor should he ever show his nose in

the room. As Philips was celebrated for skill with the
sword, the mode of vengeance was certainly unmanly, and
stung the soul of his adversary, always morbidly sensitive
to all attacks, and especially to attacks upon his person.
The hatred thus kindled was never quenched, and breathes
in some of Pope's bitterest lines.

If not a " devilish trick," this little performance was
enough to make Pope's relations to the Addison set decidedly unpleasant. Addison is said (but the story is very
improbable) to have enjoyed the joke. If so, a vexatious
incident must have changed his view of Pope's plea-
santries, though Pope professedly appeared as his defender.
Poor old Thersites-Dennis published, during the summer,
a very bitter attack upon Addison's *Cato*. He said afterwards — though, considering the relations of the men, some
misunderstanding is probable—that Pope had indirectly
instigated this attack through the bookseller, Lintot. If
so, Pope must have deliberately contrived the trap for the
unlucky Dennis ; and, at any rate, he fell upon Dennis as
soon as the trap was sprung. Though Dennis was a
hot-headed Whig, he had quarrelled with Addison and
Steele, and was probably jealous, as the author of tragedies intended, like *Cato*, to propagate Whig principles,
perhaps to turn Whig prejudices to account. He writes
with the bitterness of a disappointed and unlucky man,
but he makes some very fair points against his enemy.
Pope's retaliation took the form of an anonymous " Narrative of the Frenzy of John Dennis." [3] It is written in
that style of coarse personal satire of which Swift was a
master, but for which Pope was very ill fitted. All his

---

[3] Mr. Dilke, it is perhaps right to say, has given some reasons
for doubting Pope's authorship of this squib ; but the authenticity
seems to be established, and Mr. Dilke himself hesitates.

neatness of style seems to desert him when he tries this tone,
and nothing is left but a brutal explosion of contemptuous hatred.   Dennis is described in his garret, pouring
forth insane ravings prompted by his disgust at the success
of *Cato ;* but not a word is said in reply to Dennis' criticisms.   It was plain enough that the author, whoever he
might be, was more anxious to satisfy a grudge against
Dennis than to defend Dennis's victim.   It is not much of
a compliment to Addison to say that he had enough good
feeling to scorn such a mode of retaliation, and perspi-
cuity enough to see that it would be little to his credit.
Accordingly, in his majestic way, he caused Steele to write
a note to Lintot (August 4, 1713), disavowing all complicity, and saying that if even he noticed Mr. Dennis's criticisms, it should be in such a way as to give Mr. Dennis
no cause of complaint.   He added that he had refused
to see the pamphlet when it was offered for his inspection,
and had expressed his disapproval of such a mode of
attack.   Nothing could be more becoming ; and it does not
appear that Addison knew, when writing this note, that
Pope was the author of the anonymous assault.   If, as
the biographers say, Addison's action was not kindly to
Pope, it was bare justice to poor Dennis.   Pope undoubtedly must have been bitterly vexed at the implied rebuff,
and not the less because it was perfectly just.   He seems
always to have regarded men of Dennis's type as outside
the pale of humanity.   Their abuse stung him as keenly
as if they had been entitled to speak with authority, and yet
he retorted it as though they were not entitled to common
decency.   He would, to all appearance, have regarded an
appeal for mercy to a Grub-street author much as Dandie
Dinmont regarded Brown's tenderness to a " brock "—as
a proof of incredible imbecility, or, rather, of want of

proper antipathy to vermin. Dennis, like Philips, was
inscribed on the long list of his hatreds ; and was pursued
almost to the end of his unfortunate life.   Pope, it is
true, took great credit to himself for helping his miserable
enemy when dying in distres, and wrote a prologue to a
play acted for his benefit.   Yet even this prologue is a
sneer, and one is glad to think that Dennis was past understanding it.   We hardly know whether to pity or to
condemn the unfortunate poet, whose unworthy hatreds
made him suffer far worse torments than those which he
could inflict upon their objects.

By this time we may suppose that Pope must have
been regarded with anything but favour in the Addison
circle ; and, in fact, he was passing into the opposite
camp, and forming a friendship with Swift and Swift's
patrons.   No open rupture followed with Addison for the
present; but a quarrel was approaching which is, perhaps,
the most celebrated in our literary history. Unfortunately,
the more closely we look, the more difficult it becomes to
give any definite account of it.   The statements upon
which accounts have been based have been chiefly those
of Pope himself ; and these involve inconsistencies and
demonstrably inaccurate statements.   Pope was anxious
in later life to show that he had enjoyed the friendship of a
man so generally beloved, and was equally anxious to show
that he had behaved generously and been treated with
injustice and, indeed, with downright treachery.   And
yet, after reading the various statements made by the
original authorities, one begins to doubt whether there was
any real quarrel at all ; or rather, if one may say so, whether it was not a quarrel upon one side.

It is, indeed, plain that a coolness had sprung up
between Pope and Addison.   Considering Pope's offences

against the senate, his ridicule of Philips, his imposition of that ridicule upon Steele, and his indefensible use of Addison's fame as a stalking-horse in the attack upon Dennis, it is not surprising that he should have been kept at arm's length. If the rod suspended by Philips at Button's be authentic (as seems probable), the talk about Pope, in the shadow of such an ornament, is easily imaginable. Some attempts seem to have been made at a reconciliation. Jervas, Pope's teacher in painting—a bad artist, but a kindly man—tells Pope on August 20, 1714, of a conversation with Addison. It would have been·worth while, he says, for Pope to have been hidden behind a wainscot or a half-length picture to have heard it. Addison expressed a wish for friendly relations, was glad that Pope had not been " carried too far among the enemy" by Swift, and hoped to be of use to him at Court—for Queen Anne died on August 1st; the wheel had turned; and the Whigs were once more the distributors of patronage. Pope's answer to Jervas is in the dignified tone ; he attributes Addison's coolness to the ill offices of Philips, and is ready to be on friendly terms whenever Addison recognises his true character and independence of party. Another letter follows, as addressed by Pope to Addison himself; but here alas ! if not in the preceding letters, we are upon doubtful ground. In fact, it is impossible to doubt that the letter has been manipulated after Pope's fashion, if not actually fabricated. It is so dignified as to be insulting. It is like a box on the ear administered by a pedagogue to a repentant but not quite pardoned pupil. Pope has heard (from Jervas, it is implied) of Addison's profession ; he is glad to hope that the effect of some " late malevolences " is disappearing ; he will not believe (that is, he is strongly inclined to believe)

that the author of *Cato* could mean one thing and say
another; he will show Addison his first two books of
Homer as a proof of this confidence, and hopes that it
will not be abused; he challenges Addison to point out the
ill nature in the *Essay upon Criticism;* and winds up by
making an utterly irrelevant charge (as a proof, he says,
of his own sincerity) of plagiarism against one of Addison's
Spectators. Had such a letter been actually sent as it now
stands, Addison's good nature could scarcely have held
out. As it is, we can only assume that during 1714
Pope was on such terms with the clique at Button's,
that a quarrel would be a natural result. According
to the ordinary account the occasion presented itself in the
next year.

A translation of the first Iliad by Tickell appeared (in
June, 1715) simultaneously with Pope's first volume. Pope
had no right to complain. No man could be supposed to
have a monopoly in the translation of Homer. Tickell
had the same right to try his hand as Pope; and Pope
fully understood this himself. He described to Spence a
conversation in which Addison told him of Tickell's
intended work. Pope replied that Tickell was perfectly
justified. Addison having looked over Tickell's translation
of the first book, said that he would prefer not to see
Pope's, as it might suggest double dealing; but consented to read Pope's second book, and praised it warmly.
In all this, by Pope's own showing, Addison seems to
have been scrupulously fair; and if he and the little
senate preferred Tickell's work on its first appearance,
they had a full right to their opinion, and Pope triumphed
easily enough to pardon them. " He was meditating a
criticism upon Tickell," says Johnson, " when his adversary sank before him without a blow." Pope's per-

formance was universally preferred, and even Tickell himself yielded by anticipation. He said, in a short preface, that he had abandoned a plan of translating the whole Iliad on finding that a much abler hand had undertaken the work, and that he only published this specimen to bespeak favour for a translation of the Odyssey. It was, say Pope's apologists, an awkward circumstance that Tickell should publish at the same time as Pope, and that is about all that they can say. It was, we may reply in Stephenson's phrase, very awkward—for Tickell. In all this, in fact, it seems impossible for any reasonable man to discover anything of which Pope had the slightest ground of complaint; but his amazingly irritable nature was not to be calmed by reason. The bare fact that a translation of Homer appeared contemporaneously with his own, and that it came from one of Addison's court, made him furious. He brooded over it, suspected some dark conspiracy against his fame, and gradually mistook his morbid fancies for solid inference. He thought that Tickell had been put up by Addison as his rival, and gradually worked himself into the further belief that Addison himself had actually written the translation which passed under Tickell's name. It does not appear, so far as I know, when or how this suspicion became current. Some time after Addison's death, in 1719, a quarrel took place between Tickell, his literary executor, and Steele. Tickell seemed to insinuate that Steele had not sufficiently acknowledged his obligations to Addison, and Steele, in an angry retort, called Tickell the "reputed translator" of the first Iliad, and challenged him to translate another book successfully. The innuendo shows that Steele, who certainly had some means of knowing, was willing to suppose that Tickell had been helped by Addison. The manuscript of Tickell's work, which has been preserved, is said to prove this to be an error, and in any case there is no real ground for supposing that Addison did anything more than he admittedly told Pope, that is, read Tickell's manuscript and suggest corrections.

To argue seriously about other so-called proofs, would be waste of time. They prove nothing except Pope's extreme anxiety to justify his wild hypothesis of a dark conspiracy. Pope was jealous, spiteful, and credulous. He was driven to fury by Tickell's publication, which had the appearance of a competition. But angry as he was, he could find no real cause of complaint, except by imagining a fictitious conspiracy; and this complaint was never publicly uttered till long after Addison's death. Addison knew, no doubt, of Pope's wrath, but probably cared little for it, except to keep himself clear of so dangerous a companion. He seems to have remained on terms of civility with his antagonist, and no one would have been more surprised than he to hear of the quarrel, upon which so much controversy has been expended.

The whole affair, so far as Addison's character is concerned, thus appears to be a gigantic mare's nest. There is no proof, or even the slightest presumption, that Addison or Addison's friends ever injured Pope, though it is clear that they did not love him. It would have been marvellous if they had. Pope's suspicions are a proof that in this case he was almost subject to the illusion characteristic of actual insanity. The belief that a man is persecuted by hidden conspirators is one of the common symptoms in such cases; and Pope would seem to have been almost in the initial stage of mental disease. His madness, indeed, was not such as would lead us to call him morally irre-

sponsible, nor was it the kind of madness which is to be
found in a good many people who well deserve criminal
prosecution ; but it was a state of mind so morbid as to
justify some compassion for the unhappy offender.

One result besides the illustration of Pope's character
remains to be noticed. According to Pope's assertion it
was a communication from Lord Warwick which led him
to write his celebrated copy of verses upon Addison. Warwick (afterwards Addison's stepson) accused Addison of
paying Gildon for a gross libel upon Pope. Pope wrote
to Addison, he says, the next day. He said in this letter that he knew of Addison's behaviour—and that, unwilling to take a revenge of the same kind, he would
rather tell Addison fairly of his faults in plain words. If
he had to take such a step, it would be in some such way
as followed, and he subjoined the first sketch of the
famous lines. Addison, says Pope, used him very civilly
ever afterwards. Indeed, if the account be true, Addison
showed his Christian spirit by paying a compliment in
one of his *Freeholders* (May 17th, 1716) to Pope's Homer.

Macaulay, taking the story for granted, praises Addison's magnanimity, which, I must confess, I should be
hardly Christian enough to admire. It was however asserted at the time that Pope had not written the verses
which have made the quarrel memorable till after Addison's death. They were not published till 1723, and are
not mentioned by any independent authority till 1722,
though Pope afterwards appealed to Burlington as a
witness to their earlier composition. The fact seems
to be confirmed by the evidence of Lady M. W.
Montagu, but it does not follow that Addison ever
saw the verses. He knew that Pope disliked him ; but
he probably did not suspect the extent of the hostility.
Pope himself appears not to have devised the worst part

of the story—that of Addison having used Tickell's name—
till some years later.   Addison was sufficiently magnanimous in praising his spiteful little antagonist as it was;
he little knew how deeply that antagonist would seek to
injure his reputation.

And here, before passing to the work which afforded
the main pretext of the quarrel, it may be well to quote
once more the celebrated satire.   It may be remarked
that its excellence is due in part to the fact that, for once,
Pope does not lose his temper.   His attack is qualified
and really sharpened by an admission of Addison's excellence.   It is therefore a real masterpiece of satire, not a
simple lampoon.   That it is an exaggeration is undeniable,
and yet its very keenness gives a presumption that it is
not altogether without foundation.

> Peace to all such! but were there one whose fires
> True genius kindles and fair fame inspires;
> Blest with each talent and each art to please,
> And born to write, converse, and live with ease;
> Should such a man, too fond to rule alone,
> Bear, like the Turk, no brother near the throne:
> View him with scornful, yet with jealous eyes,
> And hate for arts that caused himself to rise;
> Damn with faint praise, assent with civil leer,
> And without sneering, teach the rest to sneer;
> Willing to wound and yet afraid to strike,
> Just hint a fault and hesitate dislike;
> Alike reserved to praise or to commend,
> A timorous foe and a suspicious friend;
> Dreading ev'n fools, by flatterers besieged,
> And so obliging that he ne'er obliged;
> Like Cato, give his little senate laws,
> And sit attentive to his own applause:
> While wits and templars every sentence raise,
> And wonder with a foolish face of praise;
> Who would not laugh if such a man there be?
> Who would not weep, if Atticus were he?

CHAPTER III.

POPE'S uneasy relations with the wits at Button's were no obstacle to his success elsewhere. Swift, now at the height of his power, was pleased by his *Windsor Forest*, recommended it to Stella, and soon made the author's acquaintance. The first letter in their long correspondence is a laboured but fairly successful piece of pleasantry from Pope, upon Swift's having offered twenty guineas to the young Papist to change his religion. It is dated December 8, 1713. In the preceding month Bishop Kennet saw Swift in all his glory, and wrote an often quoted description of the scene. Swift was bustling about in the royal antechamber, swelling with conscious importance, distributing advice, promising patronage, whispering to ministers, and filling the whole room with his presence. He finally " instructed a young nobleman that the best poet in England was Mr. Pope, a Papist, who had begun a translation of Homer into English verse, for which he must have them all subscribe ; ' for,' says he, ' the author shall not begin to print till I have a thousand guineas for him !' " Swift introduced Pope to some of the leaders of the ministry, and he was soon acquainted with Oxford, Bolingbroke, Atterbury, and many other men of high position. Pope was not disinclined to pride himself upon his familiarity with the great, though boasting at

the same time of his independence. In truth, the morbid
vanity which was his cardinal weakness seems to have
partaken sufficiently of the nature of genuine self-respect to
preserve him from any unworthy concessions. If he
flattered, it was as one who expected to be repaid in kind ;
and though his position was calculated to turn the head
of a youth of five-and-twenty, he took his place as a
right without humiliating his own dignity. Whether
from principle or prudence, he judiciously kept himself
free from identification with either party, and both sides
took a pride in supporting the great literary undertaking
which he had now announced.

When Pope first circulated his proposals for translating
Homer, Oxford and Bolingbroke were fellow-ministers, and
Swift was their most effective organ in the press. At the
time at which his first volume appeared, Bolingbroke was
in exile, Oxford under impeachment, and Swift had
retired, savagely and sullenly, to his deanery. Yet, through
all the intervening political tempest, the subscription list
grew and flourished. The pecuniary result was splendid.
No author had ever made anything approaching the sum
which Pope received, and very few authors, even in the
present age of gold, would despise such payment. The
details of the magnificent bargain have been handed down,
and give the pecuniary measure of Pope's reputation.

The Iliad was to be published in six volumes. For
each volume Lintot was to pay 200*l.*; and, besides
this, he was to supply Pope gratuitously with the copies
for his subscribers. The subscribers paid a guinea a
volume, and as 575 subscribers took 654 copies, Pope
received altogether 5320*l.* 4*s.* at the regular price, whilst
some royal and distinguished subscribers paid larger sums.
By the publication of the Odyssey Pope seems to have

made about 3500*l.* more,[1] after paying his assistants. The result was, therefore, a total profit at least approaching 9000*l.* The last volume of the Odyssey did not appear till 1726, and the payments were thus spread over eleven years. Pope, however, saved enough to be more than comfortable. In the South Sea excitement he ventured to speculate, but though for a time he fancied himself to have made a large sum, he seems to have retired rather a loser than a gainer. But he could say with perfect truth that, " thanks to Homer," he " could live and thrive, indebted to no prince or peer alive." The money success is, however, of less interest to us than the literary. Pope put his best work into the translation of the Iliad. His responsibility, he said, weighed upon him terribly on starting. He used to dream of being on a long journey, uncertain which way to go, and doubting whether he would ever get to the end. Gradually he fell into the habit of translating thirty or forty verses before getting up, and then " piddling with it " for the rest of the morning ; and the regular performance of his task made it tolerable. He used, he said at another time, to take advantage of the "first heat," then correct by the original and other translations ; and finally to " give it a reading for the versification only." The statement must be partly modified by the suggestion that the translations were probably consulted before the original. Pope's ignorance of Greek—an awkward qualification for a translator of Homer—is undeniable. Gilbert Wakefield, who was, I believe, a fair scholar and certainly a great admirer of Pope, declares his conviction to be, after a more careful examination of the Homer than any one is now likely to give, that Pope " collected the general purport of every

[1] See Elwin's Pope, Correspondence, vol. iii. p. 129.

passage from some of his predecessors—Dryden" (who only translated the first Iliad), "Dacier, Chapman, or Ogilby." He thinks that Pope would have been puzzled to catch at once the meaning even of the Latin translation, and points out proofs of his ignorance of both languages and of "ignominious and puerile mistakes."

It is hard to understand at the present day the audacity which could lead a man so ill qualified in point of classical acquirements to undertake such a task. And yet Pope undoubtedly achieved, in some true sense, an astonishing success. He succeeded commercially ; for Lintot, after supplying the subscription copies gratuitously, and so losing the cream of the probable purchasers, made a fortune by the remaining sale. He succeeded in the judgment both of the critics and of the public of the next generation. Johnson calls the Homer "the noblest version of poetry the world has ever seen." Gray declared that no other translation would ever equal it, and Gibbon that it had every merit except that of faithfulness to the original. This merit of fidelity, indeed, was scarcely claimed by any one. Bentley's phrase—"a pretty poem, Mr. Pope, but you must not call it Homer "—expresses the uniform view taken from the first by all who could read both. Its fame, however, survived into the present century. Byron speaks—and speaks, I think, with genuine feeling—of the rapture with which he first read Pope as a boy, and says that no one will ever lay him down except for the original. Indeed, the testimonies of opponents are as significant as those of admirers. Johnson remarks that the Homer "may be said to have tuned the English tongue," and that no writer since its appearance has wanted melody. Coleridge virtually admits the fact, though drawing a different conclusion, when he says that the translation of Homer has been one of the main sources of that "pseudo-poetic diction" which he and Wordsworth were struggling to put out of credit. Cowper, the earliest representative of the same movement, tried to supplant Pope's Homer by his own, and his attempt proved at least the position held in general estimation by his rival. If, in fact, Pope's Homer was a recognized model for near a century, we may dislike the style, but we must admit the power implied in a performance which thus became the accepted standard of style for the best part of a century. How, then, should we estimate the merits of this remarkable work? I give my own opinion upon the subject with diffidence, for it has been discussed by eminently qualified critics. The conditions of a satisfactory translation of Homer have been amply canvassed, and many experiments have been made by accomplished poets who have what Pope certainly had not—a close acquaintance with the original, and a fine appreciation of its superlative beauties. From the point of view now generally adopted, the task even of criticism requires this double qualification. Not only can no man translate Homer, but no man can even criticize a translation of Homer without being at once a poet and a fine classical scholar. So far as this is true, I can only apologize for speaking at all, and should be content to refer my readers to such able guides as Mr. Matthew Arnold and the late Professor Conington. And yet I think that something remains to be said which has a bearing upon Pope, however little it may concern Homer.

We—if "we" means modern writers of some classical culture—can claim to appreciate Homer far better than the contemporaries of Pope. But our appreciation involves a clear recognition of the vast difference between

F

ourselves and the ancient Greeks. We see the Homeric
poems in their true perspective through the dim vista of
shadowy centuries. We regard them as the growth of a long
past stage in the historical evolution ; implying a different
social order—a different ideal of life—an archaic conception
of the world and its forces, only to be reconstructed for the
imagination by help of long training and serious study. The
multiplicity of the laws imposed upon the translator is
the consequence of this perception. They amount to saying that a man must manage to project himself into a
distant period, and saturate his mind with the corresponding modes of life. If the feat is possible at all, it
requires a great and conscious effort, and the attainment
of a state of mind which can only be preserved by constant attention. The translator has to wear a mask which
is always in danger of being rudely shattered. Such an
intellectual feat is likely to produce what, in the most
obvious sense, one would call highly artificial work.
Modern classicism must be fine-spun, and smell rather of
the hothouse than the open air. Undoubtedly some exquisite literary achievements have been accomplished in
this spirit ; but they are, after all, calculated for the small
circle of cultivated minds, and many of their merits can
be appreciated only by professors qualified by special
training. Most frequently we can hope for pretty play-
things, or, at best, for skilful restorations which show
learning and taste far more distinctly than a glowing imagination. But even if an original poet can breathe some
spirit into classical poems, the poor translator, with the
dread of philologists and antiquarians in the back-ground,
is so fettered that free movement becomes almost impossible. No one, I should venture to prophesy, will really
succeed in such work unless he frankly accepts the im-

possibility of reproducing the original, and aims only at
an equivalent for some of its aspects. The perception of
this change will enable us to realize Pope's mode of approaching the problem. The condemnatory epithet most
frequently applied to him is "artificial;" and yet, as I
have just said, a modern translator is surely more artificial, so far as he is attempting a more radical transfor-
mation of his own thoughts into the forms of a past
epoch. But we can easily see in what sense Pope's work
fairly deserves the name. The poets of an older period
frankly adopted the classical mythology without any apparent sense of incongruity. They mix heathen deities with
Christian saints, and the ancient heroes adopt the manners
of chivalrous romance without the slightest difficulty.
The freedom was still granted to the writers of the renais-
sance. Milton makes Phœbus and St. Peter discourse in
successive stanzas, as if they belonged to the same pan-
theon. For poetical purposes the old gods are simply
canonized as Christian saints, as, in a more theological
frame of mind, they are regarded as devils. In the reign
of common sense this was no longer possible. The incongruity was recognized and condemned. The gods were
vanishing under the clearer light, as modern thought
began more consciously to assert its independence. Yet
the unreality of the old mythology is not felt to be any
objection to their use as conventional symbols. Homer's
gods, says Pope in his preface, are still the gods of
poetry. Their vitality was nearly extinct; but they
were regarded as convenient personifications of abstract
qualities, machines for epic poetry, or figures to be used
in allegory. In the absence of a true historical perception,
the same view was attributed to Homer. Homer, as Pope
admits, did not invent the gods; but he was the "first

who brought them into a system of machinery for poetry,"
and showed his fertile imagination by clothing the pro-
perties of the elements, and the virtues and vices in
forms and persons.   And thus Pope does not feel that he
is diverging from the spirit of the old mythology when he
regards the gods, not as the spontaneous growth of the
primitive imagination, but as deliberate contrivances intended to convey moral truth in allegorical fables, and
probably devised by sages for the good of the vulgar.

The old gods, then, were made into stiff mechanical
figures, as dreary as Justice with her scales, or Fame blow-
ing a trumpet on a monument.   They belonged to that
family of dismal personifications which it was customary
to mark with the help of capital letters.   Certainly they
are a dismal and frigid set of beings, though they still
lead a shivering existence on the tops of public monu-
ments, and hold an occasional wreath over the head of a
British grenadier.   To identify the Homeric gods with these
wearisome constructions was to have a more serious disqua-
lification for fully entering into Homer's spirit than even an
imperfect acquaintance with Greek, and Pope is greatly
exercised in his mind by their eating and drinking and
fighting, and uncompromising anthropomorphism.   He
apologizes for his author, and tries to excuse him for unwilling compliance with popular prejudices.   The Homeric
theology he urges was still substantially sound, and
Homer had always a distinct moral and political purpose.
The Iliad, for example, was meant to show the wickedness of quarrelling, and the evil results of an insatiable
thirst for glory, though shallow persons have thought that
Homer only thought to please.

The artificial diction about which so much has been
said is the natural vehicle of this treatment.   The set of

phrases and the peculiar mould into which his sentences were cast, was already the accepted type for poetry which aimed at dignity. He was following Dryden as his own performance became the law for the next generation. The style in which a woman is called a nymph—and women generally are "the fair"—in which shepherds are conscious swains, and a poet invokes the muses and strikes a lyre, and breathes on a reed, and a nightingale singing becomes Philomel "pouring her throat," represents a fashion as worn out as hoops and wigs. By the time of Wordsworth it was a mere survival—a dead form remaining after its true function had entirely vanished. The proposal to return to the language of common life was the natural revolt of one who desired poetry to be above all things the genuine expression of real emotion. Yet it is, I think, impossible to maintain that the diction of poetry should be simply that of common life.

The true principle would rather seem to be that any style becomes bad when it dies; when it is used merely as a tradition, and not as the best mode of producing the desired impression; and when, therefore, it represents a rule imposed from without, and is not an expression of the spontaneous working of minds in which the corresponding impulse is thoroughly incarnated. In such a case, no doubt, the diction becomes a burden, and a man is apt to fancy himself a poet because he is the slave of the external form instead of using it as the most familiar instrument. By Wordsworth's time the Pope style was thus effete; what ought to be the dress of thought had become the rigid armour into which thought was forcibly compressed, and a revolt was inevitable. We may agree, too, that his peculiar style was in a sense artificial, even in the days of Pope. It had come

into existence during the reign of the Restoration wits,
under the influence of foreign models, not as the spontaneous outgrowth of a gradual development, and had
therefore something mechanical and conscious, even when
it flourished most vigorously.   It came in with the
periwigs, to which it is so often compared, and, like the
artificial headgear, was an attempt to give a dignified or
full-dress appearance to the average prosaic human being.
Having this innate weakness of pomposity and exaggeration, it naturally expired, and became altogether ridiculous,
with the generation to which it belonged.   As the wit or
man of the world had at bottom a very inadequate conception of epic poetry, he became inevitably strained and
contorted when he tried to give himself the airs of a poet.

After making all such deductions, it would still seem
that the bare fact that he was working in a generally
accepted style gave Pope a very definite advantage.   He
spoke more or less in a falsetto, but he could at once
strike a key intelligible to his audience.   An earlier
poet would simply annex Homer's gods and fix them with
a mediæval framework.   A more modern poet tries to
find some style which will correspond to the Homeric as
closely as possible, and feels that he is making an experiment beset with all manner of difficulties.   Pope needed no
more to bother himself about such matters than about grammatical or philological refinements.   He found a ready-
made style which was assumed to be correct ; he had to
write in regular rhymed couplets, as neatly rhymed and
tersely expressed as might be ; and the diction was equally
settled.   He was to keep to Homer for the substance, but
he could throw in any little ornaments to suit the taste of
his readers ; and if they found out a want of scrupulous
fidelity, he might freely say that he did not aim at such

details. Working, therefore, upon the given data, he could enjoy a considerable amount of freedom, and throw his whole energy into the task of forcible expression without feeling himself trammelled at every step. The result would certainly not be Homer, but it might be a fine epic poem as epic poetry was understood in the days of Anne and George I.—a hybrid genus, at the best, something without enough constitutional vigour to be valuable when really original, but not without a merit of its own when modelled upon the lines laid down in the great archetype.

When we look at Pope's Iliad upon this understanding, we cannot fail, I think, to admit that it has merits which makes its great success intelligible. If we read it as a purely English poem, the sustained vivacity and emphasis of the style give it a decisive superiority over its rivals. It has become the fashion to quote Chapman since the noble sonnet in which Keats, in testifying to the power of the Elizabethan translator, testifies rather to his own exquisite perception. Chapman was a poet worthy of our great poetic period, and Pope himself testifies to the "daring fiery spirit" which animates his translation, and says that it is not unlike what Homer himself might have written in his youth—surely not a grudging praise. But though this is true, I will venture to assert that Chapman also sins, not merely by his love of quaintness, but by constantly indulging in sheer doggerel. If his lines do not stagnate, they foam and fret like a mountain brook, instead of flowing continuously and majestically like a great river. He surpasses Pope chiefly, as it seems to me, where Pope's conventional verbiage smothers and conceals some vivid image from nature. Pope, of course, was a thorough man of forms, and when he has to speak of sea or sky or mountain generally draws upon the current coin of poetic phraseology, which has lost all sharpness of impression in its long circulation. Here, for example, is Pope's version of a simile in the fourth book :—

> As when the winds, ascending by degrees
> First move the whitening surface of the seas,
> The billows float in order to the shore,
> The waves behind roll on the waves before,
> Till with the growing storm the deeps arise,
> Foam o'er the rocks, and thunder to the skies.

Each phrase is either wrong or escapes from error by vagueness, and one would swear that Pope had never seen the sea. Chapman says,—

> And as when with the west wind flaws, the sea thrusts up her waves
> One after other, thick and high, upon the groaning shores,
> First in herself loud, but opposed with banks and rocks she roars,
> And all her back in bristles set, spits every way her foam.

This is both clumsy and introduces the quaint and unauthorized image of a pig, but it is unmistakably vivid. Pope is equally troubled when he has to deal with Homer's downright vernacular. He sometimes ventures apologetically to give the original word. He allows Achilles to speak pretty vigorously to Agamemnon in the first book :—

> O monster ! mix'd of insolence and fear,
> Thou dog in forehead, but in heart a deer !

Chapman translates the phrase more fully, but adds a characteristic quibble :—

> Thou ever steep'd in wine,
> Dog's face, with heart but of a hart.

Tickell manages the imputation of drink, but has to slur over the dog and the deer :—

> Valiant with wine and furious from the bowl,
> Thou fierce-look'd talker, with a coward soul.

Elsewhere Pope hesitates in the use of such plain speak-

ing. He allows Teucer to call Hector a dog, but apologises
in a note. " This is literal from the Greek," he says, " and
I have ventured it ;" though he quotes Milton's " dogs of
hell " to back himself with a precedent. But he cannot
quite stand Homer's downright comparison of Ajax to an
ass, and speaks of him in gingerly fashion as—

> The slow beast with heavy strength endued.

Pope himself thinks the passage " inimitably just and
beautiful ;" but on the whole, he says, " a translator owes
so much to the taste of the age in which he lives as
not to make too great a compliment to the former [age] ;
and this induced me to omit the mention of the word *ass*
in the translation." Boileau and Longinus, he tells us,
would approve the omission of mean and vulgar words.
" Ass " is the vilest word imaginable in English or
Latin, but of dignity enough in Greek and Hebrew to be
employed " on the most magnificent occasions."

The Homeric phrase is thus often muffled and deadened
by Pope's verbiage. Dignity of a kind is gained at
the cost of energy. If such changes admit of some apology
as an attempt to preserve what is undoubtedly a Homeric
characteristic, we must admit that the " dignity " is often
false ; it rests upon mere mouthing instead of simplicity
and directness, and suggests that Pope might have approved
the famous emendation " he died in indigent circum-
stances," for " he died poor." The same weakness is perhaps more annoying when it leads to sins of commission.
Pope never scruples to amend Homer by little epigrammatic
amplifications, which are characteristic of the contemporary rhetoric. A single illustration of a fault sufficiently
notorious will be sufficient. When Nestor, in the eleventh
book, rouses Diomed at night, Pope naturally smoothes

down the testy remark of the sleepy warrior ; but he tries
to improve Nestor's directions.   Nestor tells Diomed, in
most direct terms, that the need is great, and that he must
go at once and rouse Ajax.   In Pope's translation we have—

> Each single Greek in this conclusive strife
> Stands on the sharpest edge of death or life ;
> Yet if my years thy kind regard engage,
> Employ thy youth as I employ my age ;
> Succeed to these my cares, and rouse the rest ;
> He serves me most, who serves his country best.

The false air of epigram which Pope gives to the fourth
line is characteristic ; and the concluding tag, which is
quite unauthorized, reminds us irresistibly of one of
the rhymes which an actor always spouted to the
audience by way of winding up an act in the contemporary drama.   Such embroidery is profusely applied by
Pope wherever he thinks that Homer, like Diomed, is
slumbering too deeply.   And, of course, that is not the
way in which Nestor roused Diomed or Homer keeps his
readers awake.

Such faults have been so fully exposed that we
need not dwell upon them further.   They come to
this, that Pope was really a wit of the days of Queen
Anne, and saw only that aspect of Homer which was
visible to his kind.   The poetic mood was not for him a
fine frenzy—for good sense must condemn all frenzy—but
a deliberate elevation of the bard by high-heeled shoes and
a full-bottomed wig.   Seas and mountains, being invisible
from Button's, could only be described by worn phrases
from the Latin grammar.   Even his narrative must be full
of epigrams to avoid the one deadly sin of dulness, and
his language must be decorous even at the price of being
sometimes emasculated.   But accept these conditions, and

much still remains. After all, a wit was still a human being, and much more nearly related to us than an ancient Greek. Pope's style, when he is at his best, has the merit of being thoroughly alive; there are no dead masses of useless verbiage; every excrescence has been carefully pruned away; slovenly paraphrases and indistinct slurrings over of the meaning have disappeared. He corrected carefully and scrupulously, as his own statement implies, not with a view of transferring as large a portion as possible of his author's meaning to his own verses, but in order to make the versification as smooth and the sense as transparent as possible. We have the pleasure which we receive from really polished oratory; every point is made to tell; if the emphasis is too often pointed by some showy antithesis, we are at least never uncertain as to the meaning; and if the versification is often monotonous, it is articulate and easily caught at first sight. These are the essential merits of good declamation, and it is in the true declamatory passages that Pope is at his best. The speeches of his heroes are often admirable, full of spirit, well balanced and skilfully arranged pieces of rhetoric—not a mere inorganic series of observations. Undoubtedly the warriors are a little too epigrammatic and too consciously didactic; and we feel almost scandalized when they take to downright blows, as though Walpole and St. John were interrupting a debate in the House of Commons by fisticuffs. They would be better in the senate than the field. But the brilliant rhetoric implies also a sense of dignity which is not mere artificial mouthing. Pope, as it seems to me, rises to a level of sustained eloquence when he has to act as interpreter for the direct expression of broad magnanimous sentiment. Classical critics may explain by what shades of feeling the aristocratic grandeur

of soul of an English noble differed from the analogous
quality in heroic Greece, and find the difference reflected
in the "grand style" of Pope as compared with that of
Homer.   But Pope could at least assume with admirable
readiness the lofty air of superiority to personal fears
and patriotic devotion to a great cause, which is common
to the type in every age.   His tendency to didactic
platitudes is at least out of place in such cases, and his
dread of vulgarity and quaintness, with his genuine feeling
for breadth of effect, frequently enables him to be really
dignified and impressive.   It will perhaps be sufficient
illustration of these qualities if I conclude these remarks
by giving his translation of Hector's speech to Poly-
damas in the twelfth book, with its famous εἰς οἰωνὸς
ἄριστος ἀμύνεσθαι περὶ πάτρης.

> To him then Hector with disdain return'd ;
> (Fierce as he spoke, his eyes with fury burn'd)—
> Are these the faithful counsels of thy tongue?
> Thy will is partial, not thy reason wrong ;
> Or if the purpose of thy heart thou sent,
> Sure Heaven resumes the little sense it lent—
> What coward counsels would thy madness move
> Against the word, the will reveal'd of Jove?
> The leading sign, the irrevocable nod
> And happy thunders of the favouring God?
> These shall I slight?   And guide my wavering mind
> By wand'ring birds that flit with every wind?
> Ye vagrants of the sky ! your wings extend
> Or where the suns arise or where descend ;
> To right or left, unheeded take your way,
> While I the dictates of high heaven obey.
> Without a sigh his sword the brave man draws,
> And asks no omen but his country's cause.
> But why should'st thou suspect the war's success ?
> None fears it more, as none promotes it less.
> Tho' all our ships amid yon ships expire,
> Trust thy own cowardice to escape the fire.

Troy and her sons may find a general grave,
But thou canst live, for thou canst be a slave.
Yet should the fears that wary mind suggests
Spread their cold poison through our soldiers' breasts,
My javelin can revenge so base a part,
And free the soul that quivers in thy heart.

The six volumes of the Iliad were published during
the years 1715—1720, and were closed by a dedication to
Congreve, who, as an eminent man of letters, not too
closely connected with either Whigs or Tories, was
the most appropriate recipient of such a compliment.
Pope was enriched by his success, and no doubt wearied
by his labours. But his restless intellect would never
leave him to indulge in prolonged repose, and, though not
avaricious, he was not more averse than other men to in-
creasing his fortune. He soon undertook two sufficiently
laborious works. The first was an edition of Shakspeare,
for which he only received 217*l*. 10*s*., and which seems
to have been regarded as a failure. It led, like his other
publications, to a quarrel to be hereafter mentioned, but
need not detain us at present. It appeared in 1725, when
he was already deep in another project. The success
of the Iliad naturally suggested an attempt upon the
Odyssey. Pope, however, was tired of translating,
and he arranged for assistance. He took into alliance a
couple of Cambridge men, who were small poets capable of
fairly adopting his versification. One of them was
William Broome, a clergyman who held several livings
and married a rich widow. Unfortunately his independence did not restrain him from writing poetry, for which
want of means would have been the only sufficient excuse.
He was a man of some classical attainments, and had
helped Pope in compiling notes to the Iliad from

Eustathius, an author whom Pope would have been
scarcely able to read without such assistance.   Elijah
Fenton, his other assistant, was a Cambridge man who
had sacrificed his claims of preferment by becoming a non-
juror, and picked up a living partly by writing and
chiefly by acting as tutor to Lord Orrery, and afterwards
in the family of Trumball's widow.   Pope, who introduced
him to Lady Trumball, had also introduced him to Craggs,
who, when Secretary of State, felt his want of a decent
education, and wished to be polished by some competent
person.   He seems to have been a kindly, idle, honourable
man, who died, says Pope, of indolence, and more immediately, it appears, of the gout.   The alliance thus
formed was rather a delicate one, and was embittered by
some of Pope's usual trickery.   In issuing his proposals
he spoke in ambiguous terms of two friends who were to
render him some undefined assistance, and did not claim
to be the translator, but to have undertaken the translation.   The assistants, in fact, did half the work, Broome
translating eight, and Fenton four, out of the twenty-four
books.   Pope was unwilling to acknowledge the full
amount of their contributions ; he persuaded Broome—
a weak, good-natured man — to set his hand to a
postscript to the Odyssey, in which only three books
are given to Broome himself, and only two to Fenton.
When Pope was attacked for passing off other people's
verses as his own, he boldly appealed to this statement to prove that he had only received Broome's help in
three books, and at the same time stated the whole amount
which he had paid for the eight, as though it had been
paid for the three.   When Broome, in spite of his sub-
servience, became a little restive under this treatment,
Pope indirectly admitted the truth by claiming only

twelve books in an advertisement to his works, and in a
note to the *Dunciad*, but did not explicitly retract the
other statement. Broome could not effectively rebuke his
fellow-sinner. He had, in fact, conspired with Pope to
attract the public by the use of the most popular name,
and could not even claim his own afterwards. He
had, indeed, talked too much, according to Pope; and
the poet's morality is oddly illustrated in a letter, in
which he complains of Broome's indiscretion for letting
out the secret ; and explains that, as the facts are so far
known, it would now be " unjust and dishonourable" to
continue the concealment. It would be impossible to
accept more frankly the theory that lying is wrong when
it is found out. Meanwhile Pope's conduct to his victims
or accomplices was not over-generous. He made over
3500*l*. after paying Broome 500*l*. (including 100*l*. for
notes) and Fenton 200*l*., that is, 50*l*. a book. The rate
of pay was as high as the work was worth, and as much as
it would fetch in the open market. The large sum was
entirely due to Pope's reputation, though obtained, so far
as the true authorship was concealed, upon something like
false pretences. Still, we could have wished that he had
been a little more liberal with his share of the plunder. A coolness ensued between the principal and his
partners in consequence of these questionable dealings.
Fenton seems never to have been reconciled to Pope,
though they did not openly quarrel and Pope wrote a
laudatory epitaph for him on his death in 1730. Broome—
a weaker man—though insulted by Pope in the *Dunciad*
and the Miscellanies, accepted a reconciliation, for which
Pope seems to have been eager, perhaps feeling some
touch of remorse for the injuries which he had inflicted.

The shares of the three colleagues in the Odyssey are

not to be easily distinguished by internal evidence. On
trying the experiment by a cursory reading I confess
(though a critic does not willingly admit his fallibility)
that I took some of Broome's work for Pope's, and, though
closer study or an acuter perception might discriminate
more accurately, I do not think that the distinction would
be easy. This may be taken to confirm the common
theory that Pope's versification was a mere mechanical
trick. Without admitting this, it must be admitted that
the external characteristics of his manner were easily caught;
and that it was not hard for a clever versifier to produce
something closely resembling his inferior work, especially
when following the same original. But it may be added
that Pope's Odyssey was really inferior to the Iliad, both
because his declamatory style is more out of place in its
romantic narrative, and because he was weary and languid,
and glad to turn his fame to account without more labour
than necessary. The Odyssey, I may say, in conclusion,
led to one incidental advantage. It was criticized by
Spence, a mild and cultivated scholar, who was professor
of poetry at Oxford. His observations, according to
Johnson, were candid, though not indicative of a powerful
mind. Pope, he adds, had in Spence, the first experience
of a critic "who censured with respect and praised with
alacrity." Pope made Spence's acquaintance, recommended him to patrons, and was repaid by warm admiration.

CHAPTER IV.

WHEN Pope finished his translation of the Iliad, he was congratulated by his friend Gay in a pleasant copy of verses marked by the usual *bonhomie* of the fat kindly man. Gay supposes himself to be welcoming his friend on the return from his long expedition.

> Did I not see thee when thou first sett'st sail,
> To seek adventures fair in Homer's land?
> Did I not see thy sinking spirits fail,
> And wish thy bark had never left the strand?
> Even in mid ocean often didst thou quail,
> And oft lift up thy holy eye and hand,
> Praying to virgin dear and saintly choir
> Back to the port to bring thy bark entire.

And now the bark is sailing up the Thames, with bells ringing, bonfires blazing, and "bones and cleavers" clashing. So splendid a show suggests Lord Mayor's Day, but in fact it is only the crowd of Pope's friends come to welcome him on his successful achievement; and a long catalogue follows, in which each is indicated by some appropriate epithet. The list includes some doubtful sympathizers, such as Gildon, who comes "hearing thou hast riches," and even Dennis, who in fact continued to growl out criticisms against the triumphant poet. Steele, too, and Tickell,—

G

> Whose skiff (in partnership they say)
> Set forth for Greece but founder'd on the way,

would not applaud very cordially. Addison, their common hero, was beyond the reach of satire or praise. Parnell, who had contributed a life of Homer, died in 1718 ;
and Rowe and Garth, sound Whigs, but friends and often
boon companions of the little papist, had followed.
Swift was breathing " Bœotian air " in his deanery, and
St. John was " confined to foreign climates " for very
sufficient reasons. Any such roll-call of friends must
show melancholy gaps, and sometimes the gaps are more
significant than the names. Yet Pope could boast of a
numerous body of men, many of them of high distinction,
who were ready to give him a warm welcome. There
were, indeed, few eminent persons of the time, either in
the political or literary worlds, with whom this sensitive
and restless little invalid did not come into contact, hostile
or friendly, at some part of his career. His friendships
were keen and his hostilities more than proportionally
bitter. We see his fragile figure, glancing rapidly from
one hospitable circle to another, but always standing a
little apart ; now paying court to some conspicuous wit, or
philosopher, or statesman, or beauty ; now taking deadly
offence for some utterly inexplicable reason ; writhing with agony under clumsy blows which a robuster
nature would have met with contemptuous laughter ;
racking his wits to contrive exquisite compliments, and
suddenly exploding in sheer Billingsgate ; making a
mountain of every mole-hill in his pilgrimage ; always
preoccupied with his last literary project, and yet finding
time for innumerable intrigues ; for carrying out schemes
of vengeance for wounded vanity, and for introducing
himself into every quarrel that was going on around him.

In all his multifarious schemes and occupations he found
it convenient to cover himself by elaborate mystifications,
and was as anxious (it would seem) to deceive posterity
as to impose upon contemporaries ; and hence it is
as difficult clearly to disentangle the twisted threads
of his complex history as to give an intelligible picture of
the result of the investigation. The publication of the
Iliad, however, marks a kind of central point in his
history. Pope has reached independence, and become
the acknowledged head of the literary world ; and it will
be convenient here to take a brief survey of his position,
before following out two or three different series of
events, which can scarcely be given in chronological order.
Pope, when he first came to town and followed Wycherley
about like a dog, had tried to assume the airs of a rake.
The same tone is adopted in many of his earlier letters.
At Binfield he became demure, correct, and respectful to
the religious scruples of his parents. In his visits to
London and Bath he is little better than one of the
wicked. In a copy of verses (not too decent) written in
1715, as a " Farewell to London," he gives us to understand that he has been hearing the chimes at midnight,
and knows where the bona-robas dwell. He is forced to
leave his jovial friends and his worrying publishers " for
Homer (damn him !) calls." He is, so he assures us,

> Still idle, with a busy air
>   Deep whimsies to contrive ;
> The gayest valetudinaire,
>   Most thinking rake alive.

And he takes a sad leave of London pleasures.

> Luxurious lobster nights, farewell,
>   For sober, studious days !
> And Burlington's delicious meal
>   For salads, tarts, and pease.

Writing from Bath a little earlier, to Teresa and Martha
Blount, he employs the same jaunty strain. "Every
one," he says, "values Mr. Pope, but every one for a
different reason. One for his adherence to the Catholic
faith, another for his neglect of Popish supersition; one
for his good behaviour, another for his whimsicalities; Mr.
Titcomb for his pretty atheistical jests; Mr. Caryll for his
moral and Christian sentences; Mrs. Teresa for his
reflections on Mrs. Patty; Mrs. Patty for his reflections
on Mrs. Teresa." He is an "agreeable rattle;" the accomplished rake, drinking with the wits, though above
boozing with the squire, and capable of alleging his
drunkenness as an excuse for writing very questionable
letters to ladies.

Pope was too sickly and too serious to indulge long in
such youthful fopperies. He had no fund of high spirits
to draw upon, and his playfulness was too near deadly
earnest for the comedy of common life. He had too
much intellect to be a mere fribble, and had not the
strong animal passions of the thorough debauchee. Age
came upon him rapidly, and he had sown his wild oats,
such as they were, while still a young man. Meanwhile
his reputation and his circle of acquaintances were rapidly
spreading, and in spite of all his disqualifications for the
coarser forms of conviviality, he took the keenest possible
interest in the life that went on around him. A satirist
may not be a pleasant companion, but he must frequent
society; he must be on the watch for his natural prey;
he must describe the gossip of the day, for it is the raw
material from which he spins his finished fabric.
Pope, as his writings show, was an eager recipient of all
current rumours, whether they affected his aristocratic
friends or the humble denizens of Grub Street. Fully to

elucidate his poems, a commentator requires to have at his finger's ends the whole *chronique scandaleuse* of the day. With such tastes, it was natural that, as the subscriptions for his Homer began to pour in, he should be anxious to move nearer the great social centre. London itself might be too exciting for his health and too destructive of literary leisure. Accordingly, in 1716, the little property at Binfield was sold, and the Pope family moved to Mawson's New Buildings, on the bank of the river at Chiswick, and "under the wing of my Lord Burlington." He seems to have been a little ashamed of the residence; the name of it is certainly neither aristocratic nor poetical. Two years later, on the death of his father, he moved up the river to the villa at Twickenham, which has always been associated with his name, and was his home for the last twenty-five years of his life. There he had the advantage of being just on the boundary of the great world. He was within easy reach of Hampton Court, Richmond, and Kew; places which, during Pope's residence, were frequently glorified by the presence of George II. and his heir and natural enemy, Frederick, Prince of Wales. Pope, indeed, did not enjoy the honour of any personal interview with royalty. George is said to have called him a very honest man after reading his Dunciad; but Pope's references to his Sovereign were not complimentary. There was a report, referred to by Swift, that Pope had purposely avoided a visit from Queen Caroline. He was on very friendly terms with Mrs. Howard—afterwards Lady Suffolk—the powerless mistress, who was intimate with two of his chief friends, Bathurst and Peterborough, and who settled at Marble Villa, in Twickenham. Pope and Bathurst helped to lay out her grounds, and she stayed there to become a friendly neighbour of Horace Wal-

pole, who, unluckily for lovers of gossip, did not become
a Twickenhamite until three years after Pope's death.
Pope was naturally more allied with the Prince of
Wales, who occasionally visited him, and became intimate with the band of patriots and enthusiasts who
saw in the heir to the throne the coming "patriot king."
Bolingbroke, too, the great inspirer of the opposition,
and Pope's most revered friend, was for ten years at
Dawley, within an easy drive. London was easily
accessible by road and by the river which bounded his
lawn. His waterman appears to have been one of the
regular members of his household. There he had every
opportunity for the indulgence of his favourite tastes.
The villa was on one of the loveliest reaches of the
Thames, not yet polluted by the encroachments of London. The house itself was destroyed in the beginning of
this century ; and the garden (if we may trust Horace
Walpole) had been previously spoilt. This garden, says
Walpole, was a little bit of ground of five acres, enclosed
by three lanes. "Pope had twisted and twirled and
rhymed and harmonized this, till it appeared two or three
sweet little lawns, opening and opening beyond one
another, and the whole surrounded with impenetrable
woods." These, it appears, were hacked and hewed into
mere desolation by the next proprietor. Pope was, indeed, an ardent lover of the rising art of landscape
gardening ; he was familar with Bridgeman and Kent, the
great authorities of the time, and his example and
precepts helped to promote the development of a less
formal style. His theories are partly indicated in the
description of Timon's villa.

> His gardens next your admiration call
> On every side you look, behold the wall !

No pleasing intricacies intervene,
No artful wildness to perplex the scene;
Grove nods at grove, each alley has a brother,
And half the platform just reflects the other.

Pope's taste, indeed, tolerated various old-fashioned ex-
crescences which we profess to despise. He admired mock
classical temples and obelisks erected judiciously at the
ends of vistas. His most famous piece of handiwork, the
grotto at Twickenham, still remains, and is in fact a
short tunnel under the high road to connect his grounds
with the lawn which slopes to the river. He describes in
a letter to one of his friends, his "temple wholly com-
prised of shells in the rustic manner," and his famous
grotto so provided with mirrors that when the doors are
shut it becomes a camera obscura, reflecting hills, river,
and boats, and when lighted up glitters with rays reflected
from bits of looking-glass in angular form. His friends
pleased him by sending pieces of spar from the mines
of Cornwall and Derbyshire, petrifactions, marble, coral,
crystals, and humming-birds' nests. It was in fact a
gorgeous example of the kind of architecture with which
the cit delighted to adorn his country box. The hobby,
whether in good taste or not, gave Pope never-ceasing
amusement; and he wrote some characteristic verses in
its praise.

In his grotto, as he declares in another place, he could sit
in peace with his friends, undisturbed by the distant din
of the world.

There my retreat the best companions grace,
Chiefs out of war, and statesmen out of place;
There St. John mingles with my friendly bowl
The feast of reason and the flow of soul;
And he whose lightning pierced the Iberian lines
Now forms my quincunx and now ranks my vines,

> Or tames the genius of the stubborn plain
> Almost as quickly as he conquer'd Spain.

The grotto, one would fear, was better fitted for frogs than
for philosophers capable of rheumatic twinges. But de-
ducting what we please from such utterances on the
score of affectation, the picture of Pope amusing himself with his grotto and his plantations, directing old
John Searle, his gardener, and conversing with the friends
whom he compliments so gracefully, is, perhaps, the
pleasantest in his history. He was far too restless and
too keenly interested in society and literature to resign
himself permanently to any such retreat.

Pope's constitutional irritability kept him constantly on
the wing. Though little interested in politics, he liked
to be on the edge of any political commotion. He appeared
in London on the death of Queen Caroline, in 1737 ; and
Bathurst remarked that " he was as sure to be there in a
bustle as a porpoise in a storm." " Our friend Pope,"
said Jervas not long before, " is off and on, here and there,
everywhere and nowhere, *à son ordinaire*, and, therefore as well as we can hope for a carcase so crazy." The
Twickenham villa, though nominally dedicated to repose,
became of course a centre of attraction for the interviewers
of the day. The opening lines of the Prologue to the
Satires give a vivacious description of the crowds of
authors who rushed to " Twitnam," to obtain his
patronage or countenance, in a day when editors were
not the natural scapegoats of such aspirants.

> What walls can guard me, or what shades can hide ?
> They pierce my thickets, through my grot they glide ;
> By land, by water, they renew the charge ;
> They stop the chariot and they board the barge :
> No place is sacred, not the church is free,
> E'en Sunday shines no Sabbath-day to me.

And even at an earlier period he occasionally retreated
from the bustle to find time for his Homer.   Lord
Harcourt, the Chancellor in the last years of Queen
Anne, allowed him to take up his residence in his old
house of Stanton Harcourt, in Oxfordshire. He inscribed
on a pane of glass in an upper room, " In the year 1718
Alexander Pope finished here the fifth volume of Homer."
In his earlier days he was often rambling about on horse-
back.   A letter from Jervas gives the plan of one such
jaunt (in 1715) with Arbuthnot and Disney for companions.   Arbuthnot is to be commander-in-chief, and
allows only a shirt and a cravat to be carried in each
traveller's pocket.   They are to make a moderate journey
each day, and stay at the houses of various friends, ending
ultimately at Bath.   Another letter of about the same
date describes a ride to Oxford, in which Pope is over-
taken by his publisher, Lintot, who lets him into various
secrets of the trade, and proposes that Pope should turn
an ode of Horace whilst sitting under the trees to rest.
" Lord, if you pleased, what a clever miscellany might
you make at leisure hours ! " exclaims the man of business ;
and though Pope laughed at the advice, we might fancy
that he took it to heart.   He always had bits of verse on
the anvil, ready to be hammered and polished at any
moment.   But even Pope could not be always writing,
and the mere mention of these rambles suggests pleasant
lounging through old-world country lanes of the quiet
century.   We think of the road-side life seen by
Parson Adams or Humphry Clinker, and of which Mr.
Borrow caught the last glimpse when dwelling in the
tents of the Romany.   In later days Pope had to put his
" crazy carcase " into a carriage, and occasionally came in
for less pleasant experiences.   Whilst driving home one

night from Dawley, in Bolingbroke's carriage and six, he
was upset in a stream.   He escaped drowning, though
the water was "up to the knots of his periwig," but he was
so cut by the broken glass that he nearly lost the use of
his right hand.   On another occasion Spence was delighted
by the sudden appearance of the poet at Oxford, "dread-
fully fatigued;" he had good-naturedly lent his own
chariot to a lady who had been hurt in an upset, and had
walked three miles to Oxford on a sultry day.

A man of such brilliant wit, familiar with so many
social circles, should have been a charming companion.
It must, however, be admitted that the accounts which
have come down to us do not confirm such preconceived
impressions.   Like his great rival, Addison, though for
other reasons, he was generally disappointing in society.
Pope, as may be guessed from Spence's reports, had a
large fund of interesting literary talk, such as youthful
aspirants to fame would be delighted to receive with
reverence; he had the reputation for telling anecdotes
skilfully, and we may suppose that when he felt at ease,
with a respectful and safe companion, he could do himself
justice.   But he must have been very trying to his hosts.
He could seldom lay aside his self-consciousness sufficiently to write an easy letter; and the same fault probably spoilt his conversation.   Swift complains of him as
a silent and inattentive companion.   He went to sleep at
his own table, says Johnson, when the Prince of Wales
was talking poetry to him—certainly a severe trial.   He
would, we may guess, be silent till he had something to
say worthy of the great Pope, and would then doubt
whether it was not wise to treasure it up for preservation
in a couplet.   His sister declared that she had never seen
him laugh heartily; and Spence, who records the saying,

is surprised, because Pope was said to have been very
lively in his youth; but admits that in later years he
never went beyond a " particular easy smile." A hearty
laugh would have sounded strangely from the touchy,
moody, intriguing little man, who could " hardly drink
tea without a stratagem." His sensitiveness, indeed,
appearing by his often weeping when he read moving
passages ; but we can hardly imagine him as ever capable
of genial self-abandonment.

His unsocial habits, indeed, were a natural consequence
of ill-health. He never seems to have been thoroughly
well for many days together. He implied no more than the
truth when he speaks of his Muse as helping him through
that "long disease, his life." Writing to Bathurst in
1728, he says that he does not expect to enjoy any health
for four days together; and, not long after, Bathurst
remonstrates with him for his carelessness, asking him
whether it is not enough to have the headache for four
days in the week and be sick for the other three. It is
no small proof of intellectual energy that he managed to
do so much thorough work under such disadvantages,
and his letters show less of the invalid's querulous spirit
than we might well have pardoned. Johnson gives a
painful account of his physical defects, on the authority
of an old servant of Lord Oxford, who frequently saw
him in his later years. He was so weak as to be unable
to rise to dress himself without help. He was so sensitive
to cold that he had to wear a kind of fur doublet
under a coarse linen shirt ; one of his sides was con-
tracted, and he could scarcely stand upright till he was
laced into a boddice made of stiff canvas ; his legs
were so slender that he had to wear three pairs of
stockings, which he was unable to draw on and off

without help.   His seat had to be raised to bring him to
a level with common tables.   In one of his papers in the
Guardian he describes himself apparently as Dick
Distich : "a lively little creature, with long legs and
arms ; a spider [1] is no ill emblem of him ; he has been
taken at a distance for a small windmill." His face, says
Johnson, was "not displeasing," and the portraits are
eminently characteristic.   The thin, drawn features wear
the expression of habitual pain, but are brightened up by
the vivid and penetrating eye, which seems to be the
characteristic poetical beauty.

It was after all a gallant spirit which got so much work
out of this crazy carcase, and kept it going, spite of all its
feebleness, for fifty-six years. The servant whom Johnson
quotes, said that she was called from her bed four times in
one night, "in the dreadful winter of Forty," to supply
him with paper, lest he should lose a thought.   His constitution was already breaking down, but the intellect
was still striving to save every moment allowed to him.
His friends laughed at his habit of scribbling upon odd
bits of paper.   "Paper-sparing" Pope is the epithet
bestowed upon him by Swift, and a great part of the
Iliad is written upon the backs of letters.   The habit
seems to have been regarded as illustrative of his economical habits ; but it was also natural to a man who was
on the watch to turn every fragment of time to account.
If anything was to be finished, he must snatch at the
brief intervals allowed by his many infirmities.   Naturally,
he fell into many of the self-indulgent and troublesome
ways of the valetudinarian.   He was constantly wanting
coffee, which seems to have soothed his headaches ; and

---

[1] The same comparison is made by Cibber in a rather unsavoury
passage.

for this and his other wants he used to wear out the
servants in his friends' houses, by "frequent and frivolous
errands." Yet he was apparently a kind master. His
servants lived with him till they became friends, and he
took care to pay so well the unfortunate servant whose
sleep was broken by his calls, that she said that she would
want no wages in a family where she had to wait upon
Mr. Pope. Another form of self-indulgence was more
injurious to himself. He pampered his appetite with
highly seasoned dishes, and liked to receive delicacies
from his friends. His death was imputed by some of his
friends, says Johnson, to "a silver saucepan in which it
was his delight to eat potted lampreys." He would always
get up for dinner, in spite of headache, when told that
this delicacy was provided. Yet, as Johnson also observes,
the excesses cannot have been very great, as they did not
sooner cut short so fragile an existence. "Two bites and
a sup more than your stint," says Swift, "will cost you
more than others pay for a regular debauch."

At home, indeed, he appears to have been generally
abstemious. Probably the habits of his parents' little
household were very simple ; and Pope, like Swift, knew
the value of independence well enough to be systematically
economical. Swift, indeed, had a more generous heart,
and a lordly indifference to making money by his writings,
which Pope, who owed his fortune chiefly to his Homer,
did not attempt to rival. Swift alludes in his letters to
an anecdote, which we may hope does not represent his
habitual practice. Pope, it appears, was entertaining a
couple of friends, and when four glasses had been con-
sumed from a pint, retired, saying, " Gentlemen I leave
you to your wine." I tell that story to everybody, says
Swift, "in commendation of Mr. Pope's abstemiousness;"

but he tells it, one may guess, with something of a rueful
countenance. At times, however, it seems that Pope could
give a "splendid dinner," and show no want of the "skill
and elegance which such performances require." Pope,
in fact, seems to have shown a combination of qualities
which is not uncommon, though sometimes called inconsistent. He valued money, as a man values it who has
been poor and feels it essential to his comfort to be fairly
beyond the reach of want, and was accordingly pretty
sharp at making a bargain with a publisher or in
arranging terms with a collaborator. But he could also
be liberal on occasion. Johnson says that his whole
income amounted to about 800*l.* a year, out of which he
professed himself able to assign 100*l.* to charity; and
though the figures are doubtful, and all Pope's statements
about his own proceedings liable to suspicion, he appears
to have been often generous in helping the distressed with
money, as well as with advice or recommendations to his
powerful friends. Pope, by his infirmities and his talents,
belonged to the dependent class of mankind. He was
in no sense capable of standing firmly upon his own legs.
He had a longing, sometimes pathetic and sometimes
humiliating, for the applause of his fellows and the
sympathy of friends. With feelings so morbidly sensitive, and with such a lamentable incapacity for straight-
forward openness in any relation of life, he was naturally
a dangerous companion. He might be brooding over
some fancied injury or neglect, and meditating revenge,
when he appeared to be on good terms; when really
desiring to do a service to a friend, he might adopt some
tortuous means for obtaining his ends, which would
convert the service into an injury; and, if he had once
become alienated, the past friendship would be remem-

bered by him as involving a kind of humiliation, and therefore supplying additional keenness to his resentment. And yet it is plain that throughout life he was always anxious to lean upon some stronger nature ; to have a sturdy supporter whom he was too apt to turn into an accomplice ; or at least to have some good-natured, easy-going companion, in whose society he might find repose for his tortured nerves.   And therefore, though the story of his friendships is unfortunately intertwined with the story of bitter quarrels and indefensible acts of treachery, it also reveals a touching desire for the kind of consolation which would be most valuable to one so accessible to the pettiest stings of his enemies.   He had many warm friends, moreover, who, by good fortune or the exercise of unusual prudence, never excited his wrath, and whom he repaid by genuine affection.   Some of these friendships have become famous, and will be best noticed in connexion with passages in his future career.   It will be sufficient if I here notice a few names, in order to show that a complete picture of Pope's life, if it could now be produced, would include many figures of which we only catch occasional glimpses.

Pope, as I have said, though most closely connected with the Tories and Jacobites, disclaimed any close party connexion, and had some relations with the Whigs. Some courtesies even passed between him and the great Sir Robert Walpole, whose interest in literature was a vanishing quantity, and whose bitterest enemies were Pope's greatest friends.   Walpole, however, as we have seen, asked for preferment for Pope's old friend, and Pope repaid him with more than one compliment.   Thus, in the Epilogue to the Satires, he says,—

Seen him I have, but in his happier hour
Of social pleasure, ill exchanged for power.
Seen him, uncumber'd with the venal tribe,
Smile without art and win without a bribe.

Another Whig statesman for whom Pope seems to have
entertained an especially warm regard was James Craggs,
Addison's successor as Secretary of State, who died whilst
under suspicion of peculation in the South Sea business
(1721). The Whig connexion might have been turned to
account. Craggs during his brief tenure of office offered
Pope a pension of 300*l.* a year (from the secret service
money), which Pope declined, whilst saying that, if in
want of money, he would apply to Craggs as a friend. A
negotiation of the same kind took place with Halifax, who
aimed at the glory of being the great literary patron. It
seems that he was anxious to have the Homer dedicated to him, and Pope, being unwilling to gratify him,
or, as Johnson says, being less eager for money than
Halifax for praise, sent a cool answer, and the negotiation
passed off. Pope afterwards revenged himself for this
offence by his bitter satire on *Bufo* in the Prologue to his
Satires, though he had not the courage to admit its obvious
application.

Pope deserves the credit of preserving his independence.
He would not stoop low enough to take a pension at the
price virtually demanded by the party in power. He was
not, however, inaccessible to aristocratic blandishments,
and was proud to be the valued and petted guest in many
great houses. Through Swift he had become acquainted
with Oxford, the colleague of Bolingbroke, and was a frequent and intimate guest of the second Earl, from whose
servant Johnson derived the curious information as to his
habits. Harcourt, Oxford's Chancellor, lent him a house

whilst translating Homer. Sheffield, the Duke of Buckingham, had been an early patron, and after the duke's death, Pope, at the request of his eccentric duchess, the illegitimate daughter of James II., edited some of his works and got into trouble for some Jacobite phrases contained in them. His most familiar friend among the opposition magnates was Lord Bathurst, a man of uncommon vivacity and good-humour. He was born four years before Pope, and died more than thirty years later at the age of ninety-one. One of the finest passages in Burke's American speeches turns upon the vast changes which had taken place during Bathurst's lifetime. He lived to see his son Chancellor. Two years before his death the son left the father's dinner-table with some remark upon the advantage of regular habits. " Now the old gentleman's gone," said the lively youth of eighty-nine to the remaining guests, "let's crack the other bottle." Bathurst delighted in planting, and Pope in giving him advice, and in discussing the opening of vistas and erection of temples, and the poet was apt to be vexed when his advice was not taken.

Another friend, even more restless and comet-like in his appearances, was the famous Peterborough, the man who had seen more kings and postilions than any one in Europe ; of whom Walsh injudiciously remarked that he had too much wit to be entrusted with the command of an army ; and whose victories soon after the unlucky remark had been made, were so brilliant as to resemble strategical epigrams. Pope seems to have been dazzled by the amazing vivacity of the man, and has left a curious description of his last days. Pope found him on the eve of the voyage in which he died, sick of an agonizing disease, crying out for pain at night, fainting away twice in the morning, lying like a dead man for a time, and in the intervals of pain giving a dinner

H

to ten people, laughing, talking, declaiming against the corruption of the times, giving directions to his workmen, and
insisting upon going to sea in a yacht without preparations
for landing anywhere in particular. Pope seems to have
been specially attracted by such men, with intellects as
restless as his own, but with infinitely more vitality to
stand the consequent wear and tear.

We should be better pleased if we could restore a vivid
image of the inner circle upon which his happiness most
intimately depended.   In one relation of life Pope's conduct was not only blameless, but thoroughly loveable. He
was, it is plain, the best of sons. Even here, it is
true, he is a little too consciously virtuous.   Yet when he
speaks of his father and mother there are tears in his
voice, and it is impossible not to recognize genuine warmth
of heart.

> Me let the tender office long engage
> To rock the cradle of reposing age,
> With lenient arts extend a mother's breath,
> Make languor smile, and soothe the bed of death,
> Explore the thought, explain the asking eye,
> And keep awhile one parent from the sky ! [2]

Such verses are a spring in the desert, a gush of the
true feeling, which contrasts with the strained and
factitious sentiment in his earlier rhetoric, and almost
forces us to love the writer.   Could Pope have preserved
that higher mood, he would have held our affections as he
often delights our intellect.

Unluckily we can catch but few glimpses of Pope's
family life ; of the old mother and father and the affec-

---

[2] It is curious to compare these verses with the original copy
contained in a letter to Aaron Hill.   The comparison shows how
skilfully Pope polished his most successful passages.

tionate nurse, who lived with him till 1721, and died
during a dangerous illness of his mother's.   The father, of
whom we hear little after his early criticism of the son's
bad "rhymes," died in 1717, and a brief note to Martha
Blount gives Pope's feeling as fully as many pages : " My
poor father died last night.   Believe, since I don't forget
you this moment, I never shall."   The mother survived
till 1733, tenderly watched by Pope, who would never be
long absent from her, and whose references to her are
uniformly tender and beautiful.   One or two of her letters
are preserved.   " My Deare,—A letter from your sister
just now is come and gone, Mr. Mennock and Charls
Rackitt, to take his leve of us ; but being nothing in it,
doe not send it. . . . Your sister is very well, but
your brother is not.   There's Mr. Blunt of Maypell
Durom is dead, the same day that Mr. Inglefield died.
My servis to Mrs. Blounts, and all that ask of me.   I
hope to here from you, and that you are well, which is
my dalye prayers ; this with my blessing."   The old lady
had peculiar views of orthography, and Pope, it is said,
gave her the pleasure of copying out some of his Homer,
though the necessary corrections gave him and the printers
more trouble than would be saved by such an amanuensis.
Three days after her death he wrote to Richardson, the
painter.   " I thank God," he says, " her death was as
easy as her life was innocent ; and as it cost her not a
groan, nor even a sigh, there is yet upon her countenance
such an expression of tranquillity, nay, almost of pleasure,
that it is even enviable to behold it.   It would afford the
finest image of a saint expired that ever painter drew,
and it would be the greatest obligation which ever that
obliging art could ever bestow upon a friend, if you would
come and sketch it for me.   I am sure if there be no very

prevalent obstacle, you will leave any common business to
do this, and I shall hope to see you this evening as late as
you will, or to-morrow morning as early, before this winter
flower is faded." Swift's comment, on hearing the news,
gives the only consolation which Pope could have felt.
" She died in extreme old age," he writes, " without pain,
under the care of the most dutiful son I have ever known
or heard of, which is a felicity not happening to one in a
million." And with her death, its most touching and
ennobling influence faded from Pópe's life. There is no
particular merit in loving a mother, but few biographies
give a more striking proof that the loving discharge of a
common duty may give a charm to a whole character. It
is melancholy to add that we often have to appeal to this
part of his story, to assure ourselves that Pope was really
deserving of some affection.

The part of Pope's history which naturally follows
brings us again to the region of unsolved mysteries. The
one prescription which a spiritual physician would have
suggested in Pope's case would have been the love of a
good and sensible woman. A nature so capable of tender
feeling and so essentially dependent upon others, might
have been at once soothed and supported by a happy
domestic life ; though it must be admitted that it would
have required no common qualifications in a wife to calm
so irritable and jealous a spirit. Pope was unfortunate in
his surroundings. The bachelor society of that day, not
only the society of the Wycherleys and Cromwells, but the
more virtuous society of Addison and his friends, was
certainly not remarkable for any exalted tone about
women. Bolingbroke, Peterborough, and Bathurst,
Pope's most admired friends, were all more or less fla-
grantly licentious ; and Swift's mysterious story shows

that if he could love a woman, his love might be as
dangerous as hatred. In such a school, Pope, eminently
malleable to the opinions of his companions, was not likely
to acquire a high standard of sentiment. His personal
defects were equally against him. His frame was not
adapted for the robust gallantry of the time. He wanted
a nurse rather than a wife ; and if his infirmities might
excite pity, pity is akin to contempt as well as to love.
The poor little invalid, brutally abused for his deformity
by such men as Dennis and his friends, was stung beyond
all self-control by their coarse laughter, and by the consciousness that it only echoed, in a more brutal shape, the
judgment of the fine ladies of the time. His language
about women, sometimes expressing coarse contempt and
sometimes rising to ferocity, is the reaction of his morbid
sensibility under such real and imagined scorn.

Such feelings must be remembered in speaking briefly
of two love affairs, if they are such, which profoundly
affected his happiness. Lady Mary Wortley Montagu
is amongst the most conspicuous figures of the time. She
had been made a toast at the Kitcat Club at the age of
eight, and she translated Epictetus (from the Latin) before
she was twenty. She wrote verses, some of them amazingly
coarse, though decidedly clever, and had married Mr.
Edward Wortley Montagu in defiance of her father's will,
though even in this, her most romantic proceeding, there
are curious indications of a respect for prudential conside-
rations. Her husband was a friend of Addison's, and a
Whig ; and she accompanied him on an embassy to Constan-
tinople in 1716-17, where she wrote the excellent letters
published after her death, and whence she imported the
practice of inoculation in spite of much opposition. A
distinguished leader of society, she was also a woman of

shrewd intellect and masculine character. In 1739 she
left her husband, though no quarrel preceded or followed
the separation, and settled for many years in Italy.
Her letters are characteristic of the keen woman of the
world, with an underlying vein of nobler feeling, perverted
by harsh experience into a prevailing cynicism. Pope had
made her acquaintance before she left England. He
wrote poems to her and corrected her verses till she
cruelly refused his services, on the painfully plausible
ground that he would claim all the good for himself and
leave all the bad for her. They corresponded during her
first absence abroad. The common sense is all on the lady's
side, whilst Pope puts on his most elaborate manners and
addresses her in the strained compliments of old-fashioned
gallantry. He acts the lover, though it is obviously mere
acting, and his language is stained by indelicacies, which
could scarcely offend Lady Mary, if we may judge her by
her own poetical attempts. The most characteristic of Pope's
letters related to an incident at Stanton Harcourt. Two
rustic lovers were surprised by a thunderstorm in a field
near the house ; they were struck by lightning, and found
lying dead in each other's arms. Here was an admirable
chance for Pope, who was staying in the house with his
friend Gay. He wrote off a beautiful letter to Lady
Mary,[3] descriptive of the event—a true prose pastoral in
the Strephon and Chloe style. He got Lord Harcourt to
erect a monument over the common grave of the lovers,

[3] Pope, after his quarrel, wanted to sink his previous intimacy
with Lady Mary, and printed this letter as addressed by Gay to
Fortescue, adding one to the innumerable mystifications of his
correspondence. Mr. Moy Thomas doubts also whether Lady
Mary's answer was really sent at the assigned date. The contrast of sentiment is equally characteristic in any case.

and composed a couple of epitaphs, which he submitted to
Lady Mary's opinion.   She replied by a cruel dose of
common sense, and a doggrel epitaph, which turned his
fine phrases into merciless ridicule.   If the lovers had been
spared, she suggests, the first year might probably have
seen a beaten wife and a deceived husband, cursing their
marriage chain.

> Now they are happy in their doom,
> For Pope has writ upon their tomb.

On Lady Mary's return the intimacy was continued.
She took a house at Twickenham. He got Kneller to paint
her portrait, and wrote letters expressive of humble ado-
ration.   But the tone which did well enough when the
pair were separated by the whole breadth of Europe, was
less suitable when they were in the same parish.   After a
time the intimacy faded and changed into mutual antipathy. The specific cause of the quarrel, if cause there was,
has not been clearly revealed. One account, said to come
from Lady Mary, is at least not intrinsically[4] improbable.
According to this story, the unfortunate poet forgot for a
moment that he was a contemptible cripple, and forgot also
the existence of Mr. Edward Wortley Montagu, and a
passionate declaration of love drew from the lady an
"immoderate fit of laughter."   Ever afterwards, it is
added, he was her implacable enemy.   Doubtless, if
the story be true, Lady Mary acted like a sensible
woman of the world, and Pope was silly as well as
immoral.   And yet one cannot refuse some pity to the

[4] Mr. Moy Thomas, in his edition of Lady Mary's letters, con-
siders this story to be merely an echo of old scandal, and makes
a different conjecture as to the immediate cause of quarrel. His
conjecture seems very improbable to me ; but the declaration story
is clearly of very doubtful authenticity.

unfortunate wretch, thus roughly jerked back into the
consciousness that a fine lady might make a pretty play-
thing of him, but could not seriously regard him with
anything but scorn.   Whatever the precise facts, a breach
of some sort might have been anticipated.   A game of
gallantry in which the natural parts are inverted, and the
gentleman acts the sentimentalist to the lady's performance
of the shrewd cynic, is likely to have awkward results.
Pope brooded over his resentment, and years afterwards
took a revenge only too characteristic.   The first of his
Imitations of Horace appeared in 1733.   It contained
a couplet, too gross for quotation, making the most out-
rageous imputation upon the   character of " Sappho."
Now, the accusation itself had no relation whatever either
to facts or even (as I suppose) to any existing scandal.   It
was simply throwing filth at random.   Thus, when Lady
Mary took it to herself, and applied to Pope through Peterborough for an explanation, Pope could make a defence
verbally impregnable.   There was no reason why Lady Mary
should fancy that such a cap fitted ; and it was far more
appropriate, as he added, to other women notorious for
immorality as well as authorship.   In fact, however, there
can be no doubt that Pope intended his abuse to reach its
mark.   Sappho was an obvious name for the most famous
of poetic ladies.   Pope himself, in one of his last letters
to her, says that fragments of her writing would please
him like fragments of Sappho's ; and their mediator,
Peterborough, writes of her under the same name in some
complimentary and once well-known verses to Mrs. Howard.
Pope had himself alluded to her as Sappho in some verses
addressed (about 1722) to another lady, Judith Cowper,
afterwards Mrs. Madan, who was for a time the object of
some of his artificial gallantry.   The only thing that can be

said is that his abuse was a sheer piece of Billingsgate, too
devoid of plausibility to be more than an expression of
virulent hatred. He was like a dirty boy who throws mud
from an ambush, and declares that he did not see the
victim bespattered.[5]

A bitter and humiliating quarrel followed. Lord Hervey,
who had been described as " Lord Fanny," in the same
satire, joined with his friend, Lady Mary, in writing lam-
poons upon Pope. The best known was a copy of verses,
chiefly, if not exclusively by Lady Mary, in which Pope
is brutally taunted with the personal deformities of his
" wretched little carcass," which, it seems, are the only
cause of his being " unwhipt, unblanketed, unkicked."
One verse seems to have stung him more deeply, which says
that his " crabbed numbers " are

> Hard as his heart and as his birth obscure.

To this and other assaults Pope replied by a long letter,
suppressed, however, for the time, which, as Johnson says,
exhibits to later readers " nothing but tedious malignity,"
and is, in fact, a careful raking together of everything
likely to give pain to his victim. It was not published
till 1751, when both Pope and Hervey were dead. In

[5] Another couplet in the second book of the Dunciad about "hap-
less Monsieur" and " Lady Maries," was also applied at the time
to Lady M. W. Montagu: and Pope in a later note affects to deny,
thus really pointing the allusion. But the obvious meaning of
the whole passage is that " duchesses and Lady Maries" might be
personated by abandoned women, which would certainly be unpleasant for them, but does not imply any imputation upon their character. If Lady Mary was really the author of a " Pop upon Pope"—a
story of Pope's supposed whipping in the vein of his own attack
upon Dennis, she already considered him as the author of some
scandal. The line in the Dunciad was taken to allude to a
story about a M. Rémond which has been fully cleared up.

his later writings he made references to Sappho, which fixed
the name upon her, and amongst other pleasant insinua-
tions, speaks of a weakness which she shared with Dr.
Johnson,—an inadequate appreciation of clean linen. More
malignant accusations are implied both in his acknowledged
and anonymous writings. The most ferocious of all his
assaults, however, is the character of Sporus, that is Lord
Hervey, in the epistle to Arbuthnot, where he seems to
be actually screaming with malignant fury. He returns
the taunts as to effeminacy, and calls his adversary a " mere
white curd of asses' milk,"—an innocent drink, which he
was himself in the habit of consuming.

We turn gladly from these miserable hostilities, disgraceful to all concerned. Were any excuse available for
Pope, it would be in the brutality of taunts, coming not
only from rough dwellers in Grub Street, but from the most
polished representatives of the highest classes, upon personal defects, which the most ungenerous assailant might
surely have spared. But it must also be granted that
Pope was neither the last to give provocation, nor at all
inclined to refrain from the use of poisoned weapons.

The other connexion of which I have spoken has also
its mystery,—like everything else in Pope's career. Pope
had been early acquainted with Teresa and Martha Blount.
Teresa was born in the same year as Pope, and Martha two
years later.[6] They were daughters of Lister Blount, of
Mapledurham, and after his death, in 1710, and the marriage of their only brother, in 1711, they lived with their

 [6] The statements as to the date of the acquaintance are contradictory. Martha told Spence that she first knew Pope as a
" very little girl," but added that it was after the publication of
the Essay on Criticism, when she was twenty-one ; and at another
time, that it was after he had begun the Iliad, which was later
than part of the published correspondence.

mother in London, and passed much of the summer near
Twickenham. They seem to have been lively young
women, who had been educated at Paris. Teresa was the
most religious, and the greatest lover of London society. I
have already quoted a passage or two from the early letters
addressed to the two sisters. It has also to be said that he
was guilty of writing to them stuff which it is inconceivable
that any decent man should have communicated to a modest
woman. They do not seem to have taken offence.
He professes himself the slave of both alternately or
together. "Even from my infancy," he says (in 1714)
"I have been in love with one or other of you week by
week, and my journey to Bath fell out in the 376th week
of the reign of my sovereign lady Sylvia. At the present
writing hereof, it is the 389th week of the reign of
your most serene majesty, in whose service I was listed
some weeks before I beheld your sister." He had suggested to Lady Mary that the concluding lines of Eloisa
contained a delicate compliment to her; and he charac-
teristically made a similar insinuation to Martha Blount
about the same passage. Pope was decidedly an economist
even of his compliments. Some later letters are in less artificial language, and there is a really touching and natural
letter to Teresa in regard to an illness of her sister's. After
a time, we find that some difficulty has arisen. He feels
that his presence gives pain; when he comes he either
makes her (apparently Teresa) uneasy, or he sees her
unkind. Teresa, it would seem, is jealous and disapproves
of his attentions to Martha. In the midst of this we find
that in 1717 Pope settled an annuity upon Teresa of 40l.
a year for six years, on condition of her not being married
during that time. The fact has suggested various speculations, but was, perhaps, only a part of some family ar-

rangement, made convenient by the diminished fortunes
of the ladies. Whatever the history, Pope gradually became attached to Martha, and simultaneously came to
regard Teresa with antipathy. Martha, in fact, became by
degrees almost a member of his household. His correspondents take for granted that she is his regular companion. He writes of her to Gay, in 1730, as " a friend—
a woman friend, God help me !—with whom I have spent
three or four hours a day these fifteen years." In his last
years, when he was most dependent upon kindness, he
seems to have expected that she should be invited to any
house which he was himself to visit. Such a close connexion naturally caused some scandal. In 1725, he defends
himself against " villanous lying tales " of this kind to his
old friend Caryll, with whom the Blounts were connected.
At the same time he is making bitter complaints of Teresa.
He accused her afterwards (1729) of having an intrigue with
a married man, of " striking, pinching, and abusing her
mother to the utmost shamefulness." The mother, he
thinks, is too meek to resent this tyranny, and Martha, as
it appears, refuses to believe the reports against her sister.
Pope audaciously suggests that it would be a good thing if
the mother could be induced to retire to a convent, and is
anxious to persuade Martha to leave so painful a home.
The same complaints reappear in many letters, but the
position remained unaltered. It is impossible to say with
any certainty what may have been the real facts. Pope's
mania for suspicion deprives his suggestions of the slightest
value. The only inference to be drawn is, that he drew
closer to Martha Blount as years went by ; and was
anxious that she should become independent of her
family. This naturally led to mutual dislike and suspicion, but nobody can now say whether Teresa pinched

her mother, nor what would have been her account of Martha's relations to Pope.

Johnson repeats a story that Martha neglected Pope "with shameful unkindness," in his later years. It is clearly exaggerated or quite unfounded. At any rate, the poor sickly man, in his premature and childless old age, looked up to her with fond affection, and left to her nearly the whole of his fortune. His biographers have indulged in discussions—surely superfluous—as to the morality of the connexion. There is no question of seduction, or of tampering with the affections of an innocent woman. Pope was but too clearly disqualified from acting the part of Lothario. There was not in his case any Vanessa to give a tragic turn to the connexion, which, otherwise, resembled Swift's connexion with Stella. Miss Blount, from all that appears, was quite capable of taking care of herself, and had she wished for marriage, need only have intimated her commands to her lover. It is probable enough that the relations between them led to very unpleasant scenes in her family ; but she did not suffer otherwise in accepting Pope's attentions. The probability seems to be that the friendship had become imperceptibly closer, and that what began as an idle affectation of gallantry was slowly changed into a devoted attachment, but not until Pope's health was so broken that marriage would then, if not always, have appeared to be a mockery.

Poets have a bad reputation as husbands. Strong passions and keen sensibilities may easily disqualify a man for domestic tranquillity, and prompt a revolt against rules essential to social welfare. Pope, like other poets from Shakspeare to Shelley, was unfortunate in his love affairs ; but his ill-fortune took a characteristic shape. He was not carried away, like Byron and Burns, by overpowering

passions. Rather the emotional power which lay in his
nature was prevented from displaying itself by his physical
infirmities, and his strange trickiness and morbid irritability. A man who could not make tea without a stratagem, could hardly be a downright lover. We may
imagine that he would at once make advances and retract
them; that he would be intolerably touchy and suspi-
cious; that every coolness would be interpreted as a deliberate insult, and that the slightest hint would be enough
to set his jealousy in a flame. A woman would feel that,
whatever his genius and his genuine kindliness, one thing
was impossible with him—that is, a real confidence in his
sincerity; and, therefore, on the whole, it may, perhaps, be
reckoned as a piece of good fortune for the most wayward
and excitable of sane mankind, that if he never fully gained
the most essential condition of all human happiness, he
yet formed a deep and lasting attachment to a woman
who, more or less, returned his feeling. In a life so
full of bitterness, so harassed by physical pain, one is glad
to think, even whilst admitting that the suffering was in
great part foolish self-torture, and in part inflicted as a
retribution for injuries to others, that some glow of feminine kindliness might enlighten the dreary stages of his
progress through life. The years left to him after the
death of his mother were few and evil, and it would be
hard to grudge him such consolation as he could receive
from the glances of Patty Blount's blue eyes—the eyes
which, on Walpole's testimony, were the last remains of
her beauty.

CHAPTER V.

In the Dunciad, published soon after the Odyssey, Pope laments ten years spent as a commentator and translator. He was not without compensation. The drudgery—for the latter part of his task must have been felt as drudgery —once over, he found himself in a thoroughly independent position, still on the right side of forty, and able to devote his talents to any task which might please him. The task which he actually chose was not calculated to promote his happiness. We must look back to an earlier period to explain its history. During the last years of Queen Anne, Pope had belonged to a " little senate " in which Swift was the chief figure. Though Swift did not exercise either so gentle or so imperial a sway as Addison, the cohesion between the more independent members of this rival clique was strong and lasting. They amused themselves by projecting the Scriblerus Club, a body which never had, it would seem, any definite organization, but was held to exist for the prosecution of a design never fully executed. Martinus Scriblerus was the name of an imaginary pedant—a precursor and relative of Dr. Dryasdust—whose memoirs and works were to form a satire upon stupidity in the guise of learning. The various members of the club were to share in the compila-

tion ; and if such joint-stock undertakings were practicable
in literature, it would be difficult to collect a more
brilliant set of contributors.   After Swift—the terrible
humourist of whom we can hardly think without a mixture of horror and compassion—the chief members were
Atterbury, Arbuthnot, Gay, Parnell, and Pope himself.
Parnell, an amiable man, died in 1717, leaving works
which were edited by Pope in 1722.   Atterbury, a
potential Wolsey or Laud born in an uncongenial period,
was a man of fine literary taste—a warm admirer of
Milton (though he did exhort Pope to put Samson
Agonistes into civilised costume—one of the most unlucky suggestions ever made by mortal man), a judicious
critic of Pope himself, and one who had already given
proofs of his capacity in literary warfare by his share in
the famous controversy with Bentley.   Though no one
now doubts the measureless superiority of Bentley, the
clique of Swift and Pope still cherished the belief that
the wit of Atterbury and his allies had triumphed over
the ponderous learning of the pedant.   Arbuthnot, whom
Swift had introduced to Pope as a man who could do
everything but walk, was an amiable and accomplished
physician.   He was a strong Tory and high churchman,
and retired for a time to France upon the death of Anne
and the overthrow of his party.   He returned, however,
to England, resumed his practice, and won Pope's
warmest gratitude by his skill and care.   He was a man
of learning, and had employed it in an attack upon Woodward's geological speculations, as already savouring of
heterodoxy.   He possessed also a vein of genuine
humour, resembling that of Swift, though it has rather
lost its savour, perhaps, because it was not salted by the
Dean's misanthropic bitterness.   If his good humour

weakened his wit, it gained him the affections of his friends, and was never soured by the sufferings of his later years. Finally, John Gay, though fat, lazy, and wanting in manliness of spirit, had an illimitable flow of good-tempered banter; and if he could not supply the learning of Arbuthnot, he could give what was more valuable, touches of fresh natural simplicity, which still explain the liking of his friends. Gay, as Johnson says, was the general favourite of the wits, though a playfellow rather than a partner, and treated with more fondness than respect. Pope seems to have loved him better than any one, and was probably soothed by his easy-going, unsuspicious temper. They were of the same age; and Gay, who had been apprenticed to a linendraper, managed to gain notice by his poetical talents, and was taken up by various great people. Pope said of him that he wanted independence of spirit, which is indeed obvious enough. He would have been a fitting inmate of Thomson's Castle of Indolence. He was one of those people who consider that Providence is bound to put food into their mouths without giving them any trouble; and, as sometimes happens, his draft upon the general system of things was honoured. He was made comfortable by various patrons; the Duchess of Queensberry petted him in his later years, and the duke kept his money for him. His friends chose to make a grievance of the neglect of Government to add to his comfort by a good place; they encouraged him to refuse the only place offered as not sufficiently dignified; and he even became something of a martyr when his *Polly*, a sequel to the *Beggars' Opera*, was prohibited by the Lord Chamberlain, and a good subscription made him ample amends. Pope has immortalized the complaint by lamenting the fate of " neglected

genius " in the Epistle to Arbuthnot, and declaring that
the "sole return" of all Gay's "blameless life " was

My verse and Queensberry weeping o'er thy urn.

Pope's alliance with Gay had various results.   Gay
continued the war with Ambrose Philips by writing burlesque pastorals, of which Johnson truly says that they
show " the effect of reality and truth, even when the intention was to show them grovelling and degraded."
They may still be glanced at with pleasure.   Soon
after the publication of the mock pastorals, the two
friends, in company with Arbuthnot, had made an adven-
ture more in the spirit of the Scriblerus Club.   A farce
called *Three Hours after Marriage* was produced and
damned in 1717.   It was intended (amongst other
things) to satirize Pope's old enemy Dennis, called "Sir
Tremendous," as an embodiment of pedantic criticism,
and Arbuthnot's old antagonist Woodward.   A taste
for fossils, mummies, or antiquities, was at that time
regarded as a fair butt for unsparing ridicule ; but the
three great wits managed their assault so clumsily as to
become ridiculous themselves ; and Pope, as we shall
presently see, smarted as usual under failure.

After Swift's retirement to Ireland, and during Pope's
absorption in Homer, the Scriblerus Club languished.
Some fragments, however, of the great design were
executed by the four chief members, and the dormant
project was revived, after Pope had finished his Homer,
on occasion of the last two visits of Swift to England.
He passed six months in England from March to August,
1726, and had brought with him the MS. of Gulliver's
Travels, the greatest satire produced by the Scriblerians.
He passed a great part of his time at Twickenham, and in

rambling with Pope or Gay about the country. Those
who do not know how often the encounter of brilliant
wits tends to neutralize rather than stimulate their
activity, may wish to have been present at a dinner which
took place at Twickenham on July 6th, 1726, when the
party was made up of Pope, the most finished poet of the
day; Swift, the deepest humourist; Bolingbroke, the most
brilliant politician; Congreve, the wittiest writer of
comedy; and Gay, the author of the most successful
burlesque. The envious may console themselves by
thinking that Pope very likely went to sleep, that Swift
was deaf and overbearing, that Congreve and Bolingbroke were painfully witty, and Gay frightened into
silence. When in 1727 Swift again visited England,
and stayed at Twickenham, the clouds were gathering.
The scene is set before us in some of Swift's verses :—

> Pope has the talent well to speak,
> But not to reach the ear;
> His loudest voice is low and weak,
> The dean too deaf to hear.

> Awhile they on each other look,
> Then different studies choose;
> The dean sits plodding o'er a book,
> Pope walks and courts the muse.

"Two sick friends," says Swift in a letter written after
his return to Ireland, "never did well together." It is
plain that their infirmities had been mutually trying,
and on the last day of August Swift suddenly withdrew
from Twickenham, in spite of Pope's entreaties. He had
heard of the last illness of Stella, which was finally to
crush his happiness. Unable to endure the company of
friends, he went to London in very bad health, and
thence, after a short stay, to Ireland, leaving behind him

a letter which, says Pope, "affected me so much that it
made me like a girl." It was a gloomy parting, and the
last. The stern Dean retired to die "like a poisoned rat
in a hole," after long years of bitterness, and finally of
slow intellectual decay. He always retained perfect confidence in his friend's affection. Poor Pope, as he says
in the verses on his own death,—

> will grieve a month, and Gay
> A week, and Arbuthnot a day ;

and they were the only friends to whom he attributes
sincere sorrow.

Meanwhile two volumes of Miscellanies, the joint work
of the four wits, appeared in June, 1727, and a third in
March, 1728. A fourth, hastily got up, was published in
1732. They do not appear to have been successful. The
copyright of the three volumes was sold for 225*l.*, of
which Arbuthnot and Gay received each 50*l.*, whilst the
remainder was shared between Pope and Swift ; and Swift
seems to have given his part, according to his custom, to
the widow of a respectable Dublin bookseller. Pope's
correspondence with the publisher shows that he was entrusted with the financial details, and arranged them
with the sharpness of a practised man of business. The
whole collection was made up in great part of old scraps,
and savoured of bookmaking, though Pope speaks complacently of the joint volumes, in which he says to Swift,
" We look like friends, side by side, serious and merry
by turns, conversing interchangeably, and walking down,
hand in hand, to posterity." Of the various fragments
contributed by Pope, there is only one which need be
mentioned here—the treatise on Bathos in the third
volume, in which he was helped by Arbuthnot. He told

Swift privately that he had " entirely methodized and in a manner written it all," though he afterwards chose to denounce the very same statement as a lie when the treatise brought him into trouble. It is the most amusing of his prose writings, consisting essentially of a collection of absurdities from various authors, with some apparently invented for the occasion, such as the familiar

> Ye gods, annihilate but space and time,
> And make two lovers happy!

and ending with the ingenious receipt to make an epic poem. Most of the passages ridiculed—and, it must be said, very deservedly—were selected from some of the various writers to whom, for one reason or another, he owed a grudge. Ambrose Philips and Dennis, his old enemies, and Theobald, who had criticised his edition of Shakespeare, supply several illustrations. Blackmore had spoken very strongly of the immorality of the wits in some prose essays ; Swift's Tale of a Tub, and a parody of the first psalm, anonymously circulated, but known to be Pope's, had been severely condemned ; and Pope took a cutting revenge by plentiful citations from Blackmore's most ludicrous bombast ; and even Broome, his colleague in Homer, came in for a passing stroke, for Broome and Pope were now at enmity. Finally, Pope fired a general volley into the whole crowd of bad authors by grouping them under the head of various animals—tortoises, parrots, frogs, and so forth—and adding under each head the initials of the persons described. He had the audacity to declare that the initials were selected at random. If so, a marvellous coincidence made nearly every pair of letters correspond to the name and surname of some contem-

porary poetaster.   The classification was rather vague,
but seems to have given special offence.

Meanwhile Pope was planning a more elaborate cam-
paign against his adversaries.   He now appeared for the
first time as a formal satirist, and the Dunciad, in which
he came forward as the champion of Wit, taken in its
broad sense, against its natural antithesis, Dulness, is in
some respect his masterpiece.   It is addressed to Swift,
who probably assisted at some of its early stages.   O
thou, exclaims the poet,—

> O thou, whatever title please thine ear,
> Dean, Drapier, Bickerstaff, or Gulliver !
> Whether thou choose Cervantes' serious air,
> Or laugh and shake in Rabelais's easy chair,—

And we feel that Swift is present in spirit throughout the
composition.   "The great fault of the Dunciad," says
Warton, an intelligent and certainly not an over-severe
critic, " is the excessive vehemence of the satire.   It has
been compared," he adds, " to the geysers propelling a vast
column of boiling water by the force of subterranean fire ;"
and he speaks of some one who after reading a book of
the Dunciad, always soothes himself by a canto of the
Faery Queen.   Certainly a greater contrast could not
easily be suggested ; and yet, I think, that the remark
requires at least modification.   The Dunciad, indeed,
is beyond all question full of coarse abuse.   The second
book, in particular, illustrates that strange delight in the
physically disgusting which Johnson notices as characteristic of Pope and his master, Swift.   In the letter pre-
fixed to the Dunciad, Pope tries to justify his abuse of
his enemies by the example of Boileau, whom he appears
to have considered as his great prototype.   But Boileau

would have been revolted by the brutal images which
Pope does not hesitate to introduce ; and it is a curious
phenomenon that the poet who is pre-eminently the representative of polished society should openly take such
pleasure in unmixed filth.   Polish is sometimes very thin.
It has been suggested that Swift, who was with Pope
during the composition, may have been directly responsible for some of these brutalities.   At any rate, as I
have said, Pope has here been working in the Swift
spirit, and this gives, I think, the keynote of his
Dunciad.

The geyser comparison is so far misleading that Pope
is not in his most spiteful mood.   There is not that infusion of personal venom which appears so strongly in the
character of Sporus and similar passages.   In reading
them we feel that the poet is writhing under some bitter
mortification, and trying with concentrated malice to sting
his adversary in the tenderest places.   We hear a tortured
victim screaming out the shrillest taunts at his tormentor.
The abuse in the Dunciad is by comparison broad and
even jovial.   The tone at which Pope is aiming is
that suggested by the " laughing and shaking in Rabelais'
easy chair."   It is meant to be a boisterous guffaw from
capacious lungs, an enormous explosion of superlative
contempt for the mob of stupid thickskinned scribblers.
They are to be overwhelmed with gigantic cachinnations,
ducked in the dirtiest of drains, rolled over and over with
rough horseplay, pelted with the least savoury of rotten
eggs, not skilfully anatomized or pierced with dexterously
directed needles.   Pope has really stood by too long,
watching their tiresome antics and receiving their taunts,
and he must once for all speak out and give them a
lesson.

> Out with it Dunciad ! let the secret pass,
> That secret to each fool—that he's an ass!

That is his account of his feelings in the Prologue
to the Satires, and he answers the probable remonstrance.

> You think this cruel ?   Take it for a rule,
> No creature smarts so little as a fool.

To reconcile us to such laughter, it should have a
more genial tone than Pope could find in his nature.
We ought to feel, and we certainly do not feel, that
after the joke has been fired off there should be some
possibility of reconciliation, or, at least, we should
find some recognition of the fact that the victims
are not to be hated simply because they were not such
clever fellows as Pope. There is something cruel in
Pope's laughter, as in Swift's. The missiles are not mere
filth, but are weighted with hard materials that bruise and
mangle. He professes that his enemies were the first
aggressors, a plea which can be only true in part; and he
defends himself, feebly enough, against the obvious charge
that he has ridiculed men for being obscure, poor, and
stupid—faults not to be amended by satire, nor rightfully
provocative of enmity. In fact, Pope knows in his better
moments that a man is not necessarily wicked because he
sleeps on a bulk, or writes verses in a garret ; but he also
knows that to mention those facts will give his enemies
pain, and he cannot refrain from the use of so handy a
weapon.

Such faults make one half ashamed of confessing to
reading the Dunciad with pleasure ; and yet it is frequently written with such force and freedom that we half
pardon the cruel little persecutor, and admire the vigour
with which he throws down the gauntlet to the natural

enemies of genius. The Dunciad is modelled upon the Mac Flecknoe, in which Dryden celebrates the appointment of Elkanah Shadwell to succeed Flecknoe as monarch of the realms of Dulness, and describes the coronation cere- monies. Pope imitates many passages, and adopts the general design. Though he does not equal the vigour of some of Dryden's lines, and wages war in a more un- generous spirit, the Dunciad has a wider scope than its original, and shows Pope's command of his weapons in occa- sional felicitous phrases, in the vigour of the versification, and in the general sense of form and clear presentation of the scene imagined. For a successor to the great empire of dulness he chose (in the original form of the poem) the unlucky Theobald, a writer to whom the merit is attributed of having first illustrated Shakespere by a study of the contemporary literature. In doing this he had fallen foul of Pope, who could claim no such merit for his own editorial work, and Pope therefore regarded him as a grovelling antiquarian. As such, he was a fit pretender enough to the throne once occupied by Settle. The Dunciad begins by a spirited description of the goddess brooding in her cell upon the eve of a Lord Mayor's day, when the proud scene was o'er,

But lived in Settle's numbers one day more.

The predestined hero is meanwhile musing in his Gothic library, and addresses a solemn invocation to Dulness, who accepts his sacrifice—a pile of his own works—trans- ports him to her temple, and declares him to be the legi- timate successor to the former rulers of her kingdom. The second book describes the games held in honour of the new ruler. Some of them are, as a frank critic observes, " beastly ;" but a brief report of the least objec-

tionable may serve as a specimen of the whole performance.   Dulness, with her court descends

> To where Fleet Ditch with disemboguing streams
> Rolls the large tribute of dead dogs to Thames,
> The king of dykes than whom no sluice of mud
> With deeper sable blots the silver flood.—
> Here strip, my children, here at once leap in ;
> Here prove who best can dash through thick and thin,
> And who the most in love of dirt excel.

And, certainly by the poet's account, they all love it as
well as their betters.   The competitors in this contest
are drawn from the unfortunates immersed in what Warburton calls "the common sink of all such writers (as
Ralph)—a political newspaper."   They were all hateful,
partly because they were on the side of Walpole, and
therefore, by Pope's logic, unprincipled hirelings, and
more, because in that cause, as others, they had assaulted
Pope and his friend.   There is Oldmixon, a hack writer
employed in compilations, who accused Atterbury of falsifying Clarendon, and was accused of himself falsifying historical documents in the interests of Whiggism ; and
Smedley, an Irish clergyman, a special enemy of Swift's,
who had just printed a collection of assaults upon the miscellanies called Gulliveriana; and Concanen, another Irishman, an ally of Theobald's, and (it may be noted) of War
burton's, who attacked the *Bathos*, and received — of
course, for the worst services—an appointment in Jamaica ;
and Arnall, one of Walpole's most favoured journalists, who
was said to have received for himself or others near
11,000*l.* in four years.   Each dives in a way supposed to
be characteristic, Oldmixon with the pathetic exclama-
tion,

> And am I now threescore ?
> Ah, why, ye gods, should two and two make four ?

Concanen, "a cold, long-winded native of the deep," dives perseveringly, but without causing a ripple in the stream :

> Not so bold Arnall—with a weight of skull
> Furious he dives, precipitately dull,

and ultimately emerges to claim the prize, "with half the bottom on his head." But Smedley, who has been given up for lost, comes up,

> Shaking the horrors of his sable brows,

and relates how he has been sucked in by the mud-nymphs, and how they have shown him a branch of Styx which here pours into the Thames, and diffuses its soporific vapours over the Temple and its purlieus. He is solemnly welcomed by Milbourn (a reverend antagonist of Dryden), who tells him to "receive these robes which once were mine,"

> Dulness is sacred in a sound divine.

The games are concluded in the second book; and in the third the hero, sleeping in the Temple of Dulness, meets in a vision the ghost of Settle, who reveals to him the future of his empire; tells how dulness is to overspread the world, and revive the triumphs of Goths and monks; how the hated Dennis, and Gildon, and others, are to overwhelm scorners, and set up at court, and preside over arts and sciences, though a fit of temporary sanity causes him to give a warning to the deists—

> But learn ye dunces ! not to scorn your God—

and how posterity is to witness the decay of the stage, under a deluge of silly farce, opera, and sensation dramas; how bad architects are to deface the works of Wren and

Inigo Jones ; whilst the universities and public schools
are to be given up to games and idleness, and the birch
is to be abolished.

Fragments of the prediction have not been entirely
falsified, though the last couplet intimates a hope.

> Enough ! enough ! the raptured monarch cries,
> And through the ivory gate the vision flies.

The Dunciad was thus a declaration of war against the
whole tribe of scribblers; and, like other such declara-
tions, it brought more consequences than Pope foresaw.
It introduced Pope to a very dangerous line of conduct.
Swift had written to Pope in 1725 : " Take care that the
bad poets do not outwit you, as they have served the good
ones in every age, whom they have provoked to transmit
their names to posterity ; " and the Dunciad has been
generally censured from Swift's point of view.   Satire, it
is said, is wasted upon such insignificant persons.   To this
Pope might have replied, with some plausibility, that the
interest of satire must always depend upon its internal
qualities, not upon our independent knowledge of its object.   Though Gildon and Arnall are forgotten, the type
" dunce " is eternal.   The warfare, however, was demoralizing in another sense.   Whatever may have been the injustice of Pope's attacks upon individuals, the moral standard
of the Grub Street population was far from exalted.   The
poor scribbler had too many temptations to sell himself,
and to evade the occasional severity of the laws of libel
by humiliating contrivances.   Moreover, the uncertainty
of the law of copyright encouraged the lower class of
booksellers to undertake all kinds of piratical enterprises,
and to trade in various ways upon the fame of well-known
authors, by attributing trash to them, or purloining and

publishing what the authors would have suppresed. Dublin was to London what New York is now, and successful books were at once reproduced in Ireland. Thus the lower strata of the literary class frequently practised with impunity all manner of more or less discreditable trickery, and Pope, with his morbid propensity for mystification, was only too apt a pupil in such arts. Though the tone of his public utterances was always of the loftiest, he was like a civilized commander who, in carrying on a war with savages, finds it convenient to adopt the practices which he professes to disapprove.

The whole publication of the Dunciad was surrounded with tricks, intended partly to evade possible consequences, and partly to excite public interest or to cause amusement at the expense of the bewildered victims. Part of the plot was concerted with Swift, who, however, does not appear to have been quite in the secret. The complete poem was intended to appear with an elaborate mock commentary by Scriblerus, explaining some of the allusions, and with "proeme, prolegomena, testimonia scriptorum, index auctorum, and notæ variorum." In the first instance, however, it appeared in a mangled form without this burlesque apparatus or the lines to Swift. Four editions were issued in this form in 1728, and with a mock notice from the publisher, expressing a hope that the author would be provoked to give a more perfect edition. This, accordingly, appeared in 1729. Pope seems to have been partly led to this device by a principle which he avowed to Warburton. When he had anything specially sharp to say he kept it for a second edition, where it would, he thought, pass with less offence. But he may also have been under the impression that all the mystery of apparently spurious editions would excite public curiosity. He adopted other devices for avoiding unpleasant consequences. It was possible that his victims might appeal to the law. In order to throw dust in their eyes, two editions appeared in Dublin and London, the Dublin edition professing to be a reprint from a London edition, whilst the London edition professed in the same way to be the reprint of a Dublin edition. To oppose another obstacle to prosecutors, he assigned the Dunciad to three noblemen—Lords Bathurst, Burlington, and Oxford—who transferred their right to Pope's publisher. Pope would be sheltered behind these responsible persons, and an aggrieved person might be slower to attack persons of high position and property. By yet another device Pope applied for an injunction in Chancery to suppress a piratical London edition ; but ensured the failure of his application by not supplying the necessary proofs of property. This trick, repeated, as we shall see, on another occasion, was intended either to shirk reponsibility or to increase the notoriety of the book. A further mystification was equally charac-teristic. To the Dunciad in its enlarged form is pre-fixed a letter, really written by Pope himself, but praising his morality and genius, and justifying his satire in terms which would have been absurd in Pope's own mouth. He therefore induced a Major Cleland, a retired officer of some position, to put his name to the letter, which it is possible that he may have partly written. The device was trans-parent, and only brought ridicule upon its author. Finally, Pope published an account of the publication in the name of Savage, known by Johnson's biography, who seems to have been a humble ally of the great man—at once a convenient source of information and a tool for carrying on this underground warfare. Pope afterwards incorporated this statement—which was meant to prove, by some palpable

falsehoods, that the dunces had not been the aggressors—
in his own notes, without Savage's name.   This labyrinth
of unworthy devices was more or less visible to Pope's
antagonists.   It might in some degree be excusable as a
huge practical joke, absurdly elaborate for the purpose,
but it led Pope into some slippery ways, where no such
excuse is available.

Pope, says Johnson, contemplated his victory over the
dunces with great exultation.   Through his mouthpiece,
Savage, he described the scene on the day of publication ;
how a crowd of authors besieged the shop and threatened
him with violence ; how the booksellers and hawkers
struggled with small success for copies ; how the dunces
formed clubs to devise measures of retaliation ; how one
wrote to ministers to denounce Pope as a traitor, and
another brought an image in clay to execute him in effigy ;
and how sucessive editions, genuine and spurious, followed
each other, distinguished by an owl or an ass on the fron-
tispiece, and provoking infinite controversy amongst rival
vendors.   It is unpleasant to have ugly names hurled at
one by the first writer of the day ; but the abuse was for
the most part too general to be libellous.   Nor would there
be any great interest now in exactly distributing the blame
between Pope and his enemies.   A word or two may be
said of one of the most conspicuous quarrels.

Aaron Hill was a fussy and ambitious person, full of
literary and other schemes ; devising a plan for extracting
oil from beech-nuts, and writing a Pindaric ode on the occasion ; felling forests in the Highlands to provide timber
for the navy ; and, as might be inferred, spending instead
of making a fortune.   He was a stage-manager, translated
Voltaire's Merope, wrote words for Handel's first composition in England, wrote unsuccessful plays, a quantity of

unreadable poetry, and corresponded with most of the literary celebrities.   Pope put his initials, A. H., under the
head of " Flying Fishes," in the Bathos, as authors who
now and then rise upon their fins and fly, but soon drop
again to the profound.   In the Dunciad, he reappeared
amongst the divers.

> Then * * tried, but hardly snatch'd from sight
> Instant buoys up and rises into light :
> He bears no token of the sable streams,
> And mounts far off amongst the swans of Thames.

A note applied the lines to Hill, with whom he had had a
former misunderstanding.   Hill replied to these assaults
by a ponderous satire in verse upon " tuneful Alexis ; " it
had, however, some tolerable lines at the opening, imitated from Pope's own verses upon Addison, and attributing to him the same jealousy of merit in others.   Hill
soon afterwards wrote a civil note to Pope, complaining of
the passage in the Dunciad.   Pope might have relied
upon the really satisfactory answer that the lines were,
on the whole, complimentary ; indeed, more complimentary
than true.   But with his natural propensity for lying, he re-
sorted to his old devices.   In answer to this and a subsequent
letter, in which Hill retorted with unanswerable force,
Pope went on to declare that he was not the author of the
notes, that the extracts had been chosen at random, that
he would " use his influence with the editors of the
Dunciad to get the note altered "; and, finally, by an
ingenious evasion, pointed out that the blank in the
Dunciad required to be filled up by a dissyllable.   This,
in the form of the lines as quoted above, is quite true, but
in the first edition of the Dunciad the first verse had
been

> H— tried the next, but hardly snatch'd from sight.

Hill did not detect this specimen of what Pope somewhere
calls "pretty genteel equivocation." He was reconciled to
Pope, and taught the poor poet by experience that his
friendship was worse than his enmity. He wrote him
letters of criticism ; he forced poor Pope to negotiate for
him with managers and to bring distinguished friends to
the performances of his dreary plays ; nay, to read through,
or to say that he had read through, one of them in manuscript four times, and make corrections mixed with elaborate eulogy. No doubt Pope came to regard a letter from
Hill with terror, though Hill compared him to Horace
and Juvenal, and hoped that he would live till the virtues
which his spirit would propagate became as general as the
esteem of his genius. In short, Hill, who was a florid
flatterer, is so complimentary that we are not surprised to
find him telling Richardson, after Pope's death, that the
poet's popularity was due to a certain " bladdery swell of
management." " But," he concludes, "rest his memory in
in peace ! It will very rarely be disturbed by that time
he himself is ashes."

The war raged for some time. Dennis, Smedley,
Moore-Smythe, Welsted, and others, retorted by various
pamphlets, the names of which were published by Pope
in an appendix to future editions of the "Dunciad," by
way of proving that his own blows had told. Lady
Mary was credited, perhaps unjustly, with an abusive
performance called a " Pop upon Pope," relating how
Pope had been soundly whipped by a couple of his
victims—of course a pure fiction. Some such vengeance,
however, was seriously threatened. As Pope was dining
one day at Lord Bathurst's, the servant brought in the
agreeable message that a young man was waiting for
Mr. Pope in the lane outside, and that the young man's

K

name was Dennis. He was the son of the critic, and prepared to avenge his father's wrongs ; but Bathurst persuaded him to retire, without the glory of thrashing a
cripple. Reports of such possibilities were circulated,
and Pope thought it prudent to walk out with his big
Danish dog Bounce, and a pair of pistols. Spence tried
to persuade the little man not to go out alone, but Pope
declared that he would not go a step out of his way for
such villains, and that it was better to die than to live in
fear of them. He continued, indeed, to give fresh
provocation. A weekly paper, called the Grub-street
Journal, was started in January, 1730, and continued
to appear till the end of 1737. It included a continuous
series of epigrams and abuse, in the Scriblerian vein,
and aimed against the heroes of the Dunciad, amongst
whom poor James Moore-Smythe seems to have had
the largest share of abuse. It was impossible, however,
for Pope, busied as he was in literature and society, and
constantly out of health, to be the efficient editor of such
a performance ; but though he denied having any concern in it, it is equally out of the question that any one
really unconnected with Pope should have taken up the
huge burden of his quarrels in this fashion. Though he
concealed, and on occasions denied his connexion, he no
doubt inspired the editors and contributed articles to its
pages, especially during its early years. It is a singular
fact—or rather, it would have been singular, had Pope
been a man of less abnormal character—that he should
have devoted so much energy to this paltry subterranean
warfare against the objects of his complex antipathies.
Pope was so anxious for concealment, that he kept his
secret even from his friendly legal adviser Fortescue ; and
Fortescue innocently requested Pope to get up evidence

to support a charge of libel against his own organ. The evidence which Pope collected—in defence of a quack-doctor, Ward—was not, as we may suppose, very valuable. Two volumes of the Grub-street Journal were printed in 1737, and a fragment or two was admitted by Pope into his works. It is said, in the preface to the collected pieces, that the journal was killed by the growing popu-larity of the Gentleman's Magazine, which is accused of living by plunder. But in truth the reader will infer that, if the selection includes the best pieces, the journal may well have died from congenital weakness.

The Dunciad was yet to go through a transforma-tion, and to lead to a new quarrel; and though this happened at a much later period, it will be most conve-nient to complete the story here. Pope had formed an alliance with Warburton, of which I shall presently have to speak; and it was under Warburton's influence that he resolved to add a fourth book to the Dunciad. This supplement seems to have been really made up of fragments provided for another scheme. The Essay on Man—to be presently mentioned—was to be followed by a kind of poetical essay upon the nature and limits of the human understanding, and a satire upon the misap-plication of the serious faculties.[1] It was a design mani-festly beyond the author's powers; and even the fragment which is turned into the fourth book of the Dunciad takes him plainly out of his depth. He was no philo-sopher, and therefore an incompetent assailant of the abuses of philosophy. The fourth book consists chiefly of ridicule upon pedagogues who teach words instead of things; upon the unlucky "virtuosos" who care for old medals, plants, and butterflies—pursuits which afforded

---

[1] See Pope to Swift, March 25, 1736.

an unceasing supply of ridicule to the essayists of the
time ; a denunciation of the corruption of modern youth,
who learn nothing but new forms of vice in the grand
tour ; and a fresh assault upon Toland, Tindal, and
other freethinkers of the day.   There were some passages
marked by Pope's usual dexterity, but the whole is
awkwardly constructed, and has no very intelligible connexion with the first part.   It was highly admired at the
time, and, amongst others, by Gray. He specially praises
a passage which has often been quoted as representing
Pope's highest achievement in his art.   At the conclusion
the goddess Dulness yawns, and a blight falls upon art,
science, and philosophy.   I quote the lines, which Pope
himself could not repeat without emotion, and which
have received the highest eulogies from Johnson and
Thackeray.

> In vain, in vain—the all-composing Hour
> Resistless falls ; the Muse obeys the Power—
> She comes ! she comes ! the sable throne behold
> Of night primeval and of chaos old !
> Before her Fancy's gilded clouds decay,
> And all its varying rainbows die away.
> Wit shoots in vain its momentary fires,
> The meteor drops, and in a flash expires,
> As one by one, at dread Medea's strain,
> The sickening stars fade off the ethereal plain ;
> As Argus' eyes by Hermes' wand oppress'd
> Closed one by one to everlasting rest ;
> Thus at her felt approach, and secret might,
> Art after art goes out, and all is night.
> See skulking Truth to her old cavern fled,
> Mountains of casuistry heaped o'er her head !
> Philosophy, that lean'd on heaven before,
> Shrinks to her second cause, and is no more.
> Physic of Metaphysic begs defence,
> And Metaphysic calls for aid on Sense !

See Mystery to Mathematics fly!
In vain! They gaze, turn giddy, rave and die.
Religion blushing veils her sacred fires
And unawares Morality expires.
Nor public flame, nor private, dares to shine;
Nor human spark is left, nor glimpse divine!
Lo! thy dread empire, Chaos! is restored;
Light dies before thy uncreating word;
Thy hand, great Anarch, lets the curtain fall
And universal darkness buries all.

The most conspicuous figure in this new Dunciad
(published March, 1742), is Bentley—taken as the representative of a pedant rampant. Bentley is, I think, the
only man of real genius of whom Pope has spoken in
terms implying gross misappreciation. With all his
faults, Pope was a really fine judge of literature, and has
made fewer blunders than such men as Addison, Gray,
and Johnson, infinitely superior to him in generosity of
feeling towards the living. He could even appreciate
Bentley, and had written, in his copy of Bentley's Milton, "*Pulchre, bene, recte,*" against some of the happier
emendations in the great critic's most unsuccessful performance. The assault in the Dunciad is not the less unsparing and ignorantly contemptuous of scholarship. The
explanation is easy. Bentley, who had spoken contemp-
tuously of Pope's Homer, said of Pope, "the por-
tentous cub never forgives." But this was not all.
Bentley had provoked enemies by his intense pugnacity
almost as freely as Pope by his sneaking malice. Swift
and Atterbury, objects of Pope's friendly admiration, had
been his antagonists, and Pope would naturally accept
their view of his merits. And, moreover, Pope's great
ally of this period had a dislike of his own to Bentley. Bentley had said of Warburton that he was a

man of monstrous appetite and bad digestion. The
remark hit Warburton's most obvious weakness. Warburton, with his imperfect scholarship, and vast masses
of badly assimilated learning, was jealous of the reputation of the thoroughly trained and accurate critic. It
was the dislike of a charlatan for the excellence which he
endeavoured to simulate. Bolingbroke, it may be added,
was equally contemptuous in his language about men of
learning, and for much the same reason. He depreciated
what he could not rival. Pope, always under the influence of some stronger companions, naturally adopted
their shallow prejudices, and recklessly abused a writer
who should have been recognized as amongst the most
effective combatants against dulness.

Bentley died a few months after the publication of the
Dunciad. But Pope found a living antagonist, who
succeeded in giving him pain enough to gratify the
vilified dunces. This was Colley Cibber—most lively
and mercurial of actors—author of some successful plays,
with too little stuff in them for permanence, and of an
Apology for his own Life, which is still exceedingly
amusing as well as useful for the history of the stage.
He was now approaching seventy, though he was to
survive Pope for thirteen years, and as good-tempered a
specimen of the lively, if not too particular, old man of
the world as could well have been found. Pope owed
him a grudge. Cibber, in playing the *Rehearsal*, had
introduced some ridicule of the unlucky *Three Hours
after Marriage*. Pope, he says, came behind the scenes
foaming and choking with fury, and forbidding Cibber
ever to repeat the insult. Cibber laughed at him, said
that he would repeat it as long as the *Rehearsal* was
performed, and kept his word. Pope took his revenge

by many incidental hits at Cibber, and Cibber made a good-humoured reference to this abuse in the Apology. Hereupon Pope, in the new Dunciad, described him as reclining on the lap of the goddess, and added various personalities in the notes. Cibber straightway published a letter to Pope, the more cutting because still in perfect good-humour, and told the story about the original quarrel. He added an irritating anecdote in order to provoke the poet still further. It described Pope as introduced by Cibber and Lord Warwick to very bad company. The story was one which could only be told by a graceless old representative of the old school of comedy, but it hit its mark. The two Richardsons once found Pope reading one of Cibber's pamphlets. He said, "These things are my diversion;" but they saw his features writhing with anguish, and young Richardson, as they went home, observed to his father that he hoped to be preserved from such diversions as Pope had enjoyed. The poet resolved to avenge himself, and he did it to the lasting injury of his poem. He dethroned Theobald, who, as a plodding antiquarian, was an excellent exponent of dulness, and installed Cibber in in his place, who might be a representative of folly, but was as little of a dullard as Pope himself. The consequent alterations make the hero of the poem a thoroughly incongruous figure, and greatly injure the general design. The poem appeared in this form in 1743, with a ponderous prefatory discourse by Ricardus Aristarchus, contributed by the faithful Warburton, and illustrating his ponderous vein of elephantine pleasantry.

Pope was nearing the grave, and many of his victims had gone before him. It was a melancholy employment for an invalid, breaking down visibly month by month;

and one might fancy that the eminent Christian divine
might have used his influence to better purpose than in
fanning the dying flame, and adding the strokes of his
bludgeon to the keen stabs of Pope's stiletto. In the
fourteen years which had elapsed since the first Dunciad, Pope had found less unworthy employment for his
pen ; but, before dealing with the works produced at this
time, which include some of his highest achievements, I
must tell a story which is in some ways a natural supplement to the war with the dunces. In describing
Pope's entangled history, it seems most convenient to
follow each separate line of discharge of his multifarious
energy, rather than to adhere to chronological order.

CHAPTER VI.[1]

I HAVE now to describe one of the most singular series of transactions to be found in the annals of literature. A complete knowledge of their various details has only been obtained by recent researches. I cannot follow within my limits of space all the ins and outs of the complicated labyrinth of more than diplomatic trickery which those researches have revealed, though I hope to render the main facts sufficiently intelligible. It is painful to track the strange deceptions of a man of genius as a detective unravels the misdeeds of an accomplished swindler; but without telling the story at some length, it is impossible to give a faithful exhibition of Pope's character.

In the year 1726, when Pope had just finished his labours upon Homer, Curll published the juvenile letters to Cromwell. There was no mystery about this transaction. Curll was the chief of all piratical booksellers, and versed in every dirty trick of the Grub-street trade. He is described in that mad book, Amory's *John Buncle*, as tall, thin, ungainly, white-faced, with light grey goggle

---

[1] The evidence by which the statements in this chapter are supported is fully set forth in Mr. Elwin's edition of Pope's Works, Vol. I., and in the notes to the Orrery Correspondence in the third volume of letters.

eyes, purblind, splay-footed, and "baker-kneed." According to the same queer authority, who professes to have lodged in Curll's house, he was drunk, as often as he could drink for nothing, and intimate in every London haunt of vice. " His translators lay three in a bed at the Pewter Platter Inn in Holborn," and helped to compile his indecent, piratical, and catchpenny productions. He had lost his ears for some obscene publication ; but Amory adds, "to his glory," that he died "as great a penitent as ever expired." He had one strong point as an antagonist. Having no character to lose, he could reveal his own practices without a blush, if the revelation injured others.

Pope had already come into collision with this awkward antagonist. In 1716 Curll threatened to publish the Town Eclogues, burlesques upon Ambrose Philips, written by Lady Mary, with the help of Pope and perhaps Gay. Pope, with Lintot, had a meeting with Curll in the hopes of suppressing a publication calculated to injure his friends. The party had some wine, and Curll on going home was very sick. He declared—and there are reasons for believing his story—that Pope had given him an emetic, by way of coarse practical joke. Pope, at any rate, took advantage of the accident to write a couple of squibs upon Curll, recording the bookseller's ravings under the action of the drug, as he had described the ravings of Dennis provoked by Cato. Curll had his revenge afterwards ; but meanwhile he wanted no extraneous motive to induce him to publish the Cromwell letters. Cromwell had given the letters to a mistress, who fell into distress and sold them to Curll for ten guineas.

The correspondence was received with some favour, and suggested to Pope a new mode of gratifying his vanity. An occasion soon offered itself. Theobald, the hero of

the Dunciad, edited in 1728 the posthumous works of
Wycherley. Pope extracted from this circumstance a
far-fetched excuse for publishing the Wycherley correspondence. He said that it was due to Wycherley's
memory to prove, by the publication of their correspondence, that the posthumous publication of the works
was opposed to their author's wishes. As a matter of
fact the letters have no tendency to prove anything of
the kind, or rather, they support the opposite theory ;
but poor Pope was always a hand-to-mouth liar, and
took the first pretext that offered, without caring for
consistency or confirmation. His next step was to
write to his friend, Lord Oxford, son of Queen Anne's
minister. Oxford was a weak, good-natured man. By
cultivating a variety of expensive tastes, without the
knowledge to guide them, he managed to run through a
splendid fortune and die in embarrassment. His famous
library was one of his special hobbies. Pope now applied
to him to allow the Wycherley letters to be deposited in the
library, and further requested that the fact of their being
in this quasi-public place might be mentioned in the preface as a guarantee of their authenticity. Oxford consented, and Pope quietly took a further step without
authority. He told Oxford that he had decided to make
his publishers say that copies of the letters had been obtained from Lord Oxford. He told the same story to
Swift, speaking of the " connivance " of his noble friend,
and adding that, though he did not himself " much approve " of the publication, he was not ashamed of it. He
thus ingeniously intimated that the correspondence, which
he had himself carefully prepared and sent to press, had
been printed without his consent by the officious zeal of
Oxford and the booksellers.

The book (which was called the second volume of
Wycherley's works) has entirely disappeared. It was advertised at the time, but not a single copy is known to
exist. One cause of this disappearance now appears to
be that it had no sale at first, and that Pope preserved the
sheets for use in a more elaborate device which followed.
Oxford probably objected to the misuse of his name, as
the fiction which made him responsible was afterwards
dropped. Pope found, or thought that he had found, on
the next occasion, a more convenient cat's-paw. Curll, it
could not be doubted, would snatch at any chance of publishing more correspondence ; and, as Pope was anxious
to have his letters stolen and Curll was ready to steal, the
one thing necessary was a convenient go-between, who
could be disowned or altogether concealed. Pope went systematically to work. He began by writing to his friends,
begging them to return his letters. After Curll's piracy,
he declared, he could not feel himself safe, and should be
unhappy till he had the letters in his own custody. Letters were sent in, though in some cases with reluctance ;
and Caryll, in particular, who had the largest number,
privately took copies before returning them (a measure
which ultimately secured the detection of many of Pope's
manœuvres). This, however, was unknown to Pope.
He had the letters copied out ; after (according to his own
stating) burning three-fourths of them, and (as we are
now aware) carefully editing the remainder, he had the
copy deposited in Lord Oxford's library. His object was,
as he said, partly to have documents ready in case of the
revival of scandals, and partly to preserve the memory of
his friendships. The next point was to get these letters
stolen. For this purpose he created a man of straw, a
mysterious " P. T.," who could be personated on occasion

by some of the underlings employed in the underground
transactions connected with the Dunciad and the Grub-
street Journal. P. T. began by writing to Curll in
1733, and offering to sell him a collection of Pope's
letters. The negotiation went off for a time, because P. T.
insisted upon Curll's first committing himself by publishing an advertisement, declaring himself to be already in
possession of the-originals. Curll was too wary to commit
himself to such a statement, which would have made him
responsible for the theft; or, perhaps, have justified Pope
in publishing the originals in self-defence. The matter
slept till March 1735, when Curll wrote to Pope pro-
posing a cessation of hostilities, and as a proof of goodwill
sending him the old P. T. advertisement. This step fell
in so happily with Pope's designs that it has been suggested
that Curll was prompted in some indirect manner by one
of Pope's agents. Pope, at any rate, turned it to account.
He at once published an insulting advertisement. Curll
(he said in this manifesto) had pretended to have had the
offer from P. T. of a large collection of Pope's letters;
Pope knew nothing of P. T., believed the letters to be
forgeries, and would take no more trouble in the matter.
Whilst Curll was presumably smarting under this summary slap on the face, the insidious P. T. stepped in once
more. P. T. now said that he was in possession of the
printed sheets of the correspondence, and the negotiation
went on swimmingly. Curll put out the required advertisement; a " short, squat " man, in a clergyman's gown
and with barrister's bands, calling himself Smythe, came
to his house at night as P. T.'s agent, and showed him
some printed sheets and original letters; the bargain was
struck; 240 copies of the book were delivered, and it
was published on May 12th.

So far the plot had succeeded. Pope had printed his own correspondence, and had tricked Curll into publishing the book piratically, whilst the public was quite prepared to believe that Curll had performed a new piratical feat. Pope, however, was now bound to shriek as loudly as he could at the outrage under which he was suffering. He should have been prepared also to answer an obvious question. Every one would naturally inquire how Curll had procured the letters, which by Pope's own account were safely deposited in Lord Oxford's library. Without, as it would seem, properly weighing the difficulty of meeting this demand, Pope called out loudly for vengeance. When the Dunciad appeared, he had applied (as I have said) for an injunction in Chancery, and had at the same time secured the failure of his application. The same device was tried in a still more imposing fashion. The House of Lords had recently decided that it was a breach of privilege to publish a peer's letters without his consent. Pope availed himself of this rule to fire the most sounding of blank shots across the path of the piratical Curll. He was as anxious to allow the publication, as to demand its suppression in the most emphatic manner. Accordingly he got his friend, Lord Ilay, to call the attention of the peers to Curll's advertisement, which was so worded as to imply that there were in the book letters from, as well as to, peers. Pope himself attended the house " to stimulate the resentment of his friends." The book was at once seized by a messenger, and Curll ordered to attend the next day. But on examination it immediately turned out that it contained no letters from peers, and the whole farce would have ended at once but for a further trick. Lord Ilay said that a certain letter to Jervas contained a reflection upon Lord Burlington. Now the letter was found in a first batch of fifty copies sent to Curll, and which had been sold before the appearance of the Lords' messenger. But the letter had been suppressed in a second batch of 190 copies, which the messenger was just in time to seize. Pope had of course foreseen and prepared this result.

The whole proceeding in the Lords was thus rendered abortive. The books were restored to Curll, and the sale continued. But the device meanwhile had recoiled upon its author; the very danger against which he should have guarded himself had now occurred. How were the letters procured? Not till Curll was coming up for examination does it seem to have occurred to Pope that the Lords would inevitably ask the awkward question. He then saw that Curll's answer might lead to a discovery. He wrote a letter to Curll (in Smythe's name) intended to meet the difficulty. He entreated Curll to take the whole of the responsibility of procuring the letters upon himself, and by way of inducement held out hopes of another volume of correspondence. In a second note he tried to throw Curll off the scent of another significant little fact. The sheets (as I have mentioned) were partly made up from the volume of Wycherley correspondence;[2] this would give a clue to further inquiries; P. T. therefore allowed Smythe to say (ostensibly to show his confidence in Curll) that he (P. T.) had been employed in getting up the former volume, and had had some additional sheets struck off for himself, to which he had added letters subsequently obtained. The letter was a signal blunder. Curll saw at once that it put the game in his hands. He was not going to tell lies to please the slippery P. T.,

[2] This is proved by a note referring to " the present edition of the posthumous works of Mr. Wycherley," which, by an oversight, was allowed to remain in the Curll volume.

or the short squat lawyer-clergyman. He had begun to
see through the whole manœuvre. He went straight off
to the Lords' committee, told the whole story, and produced as a voucher the letters in which P. T. begged for
secrecy. Curll's word was good for little by itself, but
his story hung together and the letter confirmed it. And
if, as now seemed clear, Curll was speaking the truth, the
question remained, who was P. T., and how did he get
the letters? The answer, as Pope must have felt, was
only too clear.

But Curll now took the offensive. In reply to another
letter from Smythe, complaining of his evidence, he went
roundly to work ; he said that he should at once publish
all the correspondence. P. T. had prudently asked
for the return of his letters ; but Curll had kept copies,
and was prepared to swear to their fidelity. Accordingly
he soon advertised what was called the *Initial Correspondence*. Pope was now caught in his own trap. He
had tried to avert suspicion by publicly offering a reward
to Smythe and P. T., if they would "discover the
whole affair." The letters, as he admitted, must have
been procured either from his own library or from Lord
Oxford's. The correspondence to be published by Curll
would help to identify the mysterious appropriators, and
whatever excuses could be made ought now to be forth-
coming. Pope adopted a singular plan. It was announced that the clergyman concerned with P. T. and
Curll had "discovered the whole transaction." A narrative was forthwith published to anticipate Curll and to
clear up the mystery. If good for anything, it should
have given, or helped to give, the key to the great puzzle
—the mode of obtaining the letters. There was nothing
else for Smythe or P. T. to "discover." Readers must

have been strangely disappointed on finding not a single
word to throw light upon this subject, and merely a long
account of the negotiations between Curll and P. T.
The narrative might serve to distract attention from the
main point, which it clearly did nothing to elucidate.
But Curll now stated his own case. He reprinted the
narrative with some pungent notes ; he gave in full some
letters omitted by P. T., and he added a story which
was most unpleasantly significant.   P. T. had spoken,
as I have said, of his connexion with the Wycherley
volume. The object of this statement was to get rid of an
awkward bit of evidence.   But Curll now announced, on
the authority of Gilliver, the publisher of the volume,
that Pope had himself bought up the remaining sheets.
The inference was clear. Unless the story could be con-
tradicted, and it never was, Pope was himself the thief.
The sheets common to the two volumes had been traced
to his possession. Nor was there a word in the P. T.
narrative to diminish the force of these presumptions.
Indeed it was curiously inconsistent, for it vaguely accused Curll of stealing the letters himself, whilst in the
same breath it told how he had bought them from P. T.
In fact, P. T. was beginning to resolve himself into
thin air, like the phantom in the Dunciad. As he
vanished, it required no great acuteness to distinguish
behind him the features of his ingenious creator.   It
was already believed at the time that the whole affair was
an elaborate contrivance of Pope's, and subsequent revela-
tions have demonstrated the truth of the hypothesis.
Even the go-between, Smythe, was identified as one
James Worsdale, a painter, actor, and author, of the
Bohemian variety.

Though Curll had fairly won the game, and Pope's

L

intrigue was even at the time sufficiently exposed, it
seems to have given less scandal than might have been
expected. Probably it was suspected only in literary
circles, and perhaps it might be thought that, silly as was
the elaborate device, the disreputable Curll was fair game
for his natural enemy. Indeed, such is the irony of fate,
Pope won credit with simple people. The effect of the
publication, as Johnson tells us, was to fill the nation
with praises of the admirable moral qualities revealed in
Pope's letters. Amongst the admirers was Ralph Allen,
who had made a large fortune by farming the cross-
posts. His princely benevolence and sterling worth
were universally admitted, and have been immortalized
by the best contemporary judge of character. He was
the original of Fielding's Allworthy. Like that excellent person, he seems to have had the common weakness
of good men in taking others too easily at their own
valuation. Pope imposed upon him just as Blifil imposed
upon his representative. He was so much pleased with the
correspondence, that he sought Pope's acquaintance, and
offered to publish a genuine edition at his own expense.
An authoritative edition appeared accordingly in 1737.
Pope preferred to publish by subscription, which does not
seem to have filled very rapidly, though the work ultimately made a fair profit. Pope's underhand manœuvres
were abundantly illustrated in the history of this new
edition. It is impossible to give the details; but I may
briefly state that he was responsible for a nominally
spurious edition which appeared directly after, and
was simply a reproduction of, Curll's publication. Although he complained of the garbling and interpolations
supposed to have been due to the wicked Curll or
the phantom P. T., and although he omitted in his

avowed edition certain letters which had given offence, he
nevertheless substantially reproduced in it Curll's version
of the letters.   As this differs from the originals which
have been preserved, Pope thus gave an additional proof
that he was really responsible for Curll's supposed
garbling.   This evidence was adduced with conclusive
force by Bowles in a later controversy, and would be
enough by itself to convict Pope of the imputed deception.   Finally, it may be added that Pope's delay in producing his own edition is explained by the fact that it
contained many falsifications of his correspondence with
Caryll, and that he delayed the acknowledgment of the
genuine character of the letters until Caryll's death
removed the danger of detection.

The whole of this elaborate machinery was devised in
order that Pope might avoid the ridicule of publishing
his own correspondence.   There had been few examples
of a similar publication of private letters ; and Pope's
volume, according to Johnson, did not attract very much
attention.   This is, perhaps, hardly consistent with Johnson's other assertion that it filled the nation with
praises of his virtue.   In any case it stimulated his appetite for such praises, and led him to a fresh intrigue, more
successful and also more disgraceful.   The device originally
adopted in publishing the Dunciad apparently suggested
part of the new plot.   The letters hitherto published did
not include the most interesting correspondence in which
Pope had been engaged.   He had been in the habit of
writing to Swift since their first acquaintance, and Bolingbroke had occasionally joined him.   These letters, which
connected Pope with two of his most famous contemporaries, would be far more interesting than the letters to
Cromwell or Wycherley, or even than the letters addressed

to Addison and Steele, which were mere stilted fabrications. How could they be got before the world, and in
such a way as to conceal his own complicity?

Pope had told Swift (in 1730) that he had kept some
of the letters in a volume for his own secret satisfaction;
and Swift had preserved all Pope's letters along with
those of other distinguished men. Here was an attractive
booty for such parties as the unprincipled Curll! In
1735 Curll had committed his wicked piracy, and Pope
pressed Swift to return his letters, in order to "secure
him against that rascal printer." The entreaties were
often renewed, but Swift for some reason turned his deaf
ear to the suggestion. He promised, indeed (Sept. 3,
1735), that the letters should be burnt—a most effectual
security against republication, but one not at all to Pope's
taste. Pope then admitted that, having been forced to
publish some of his other letters, he should like to make
use of some of those to Swift, as none would be more
honourable to him. Nay, he says, he meant to erect such
a minute monument of their friendship as would put to
shame all ancient memorials of the same kind.[3] This
avowal of his intention to publish did not conciliate
Swift. Curll next published in 1736 a couple of letters
to Swift, and Pope took advantage of this publication
(perhaps he had indirectly supplied Curll with copies)
to urge upon Swift the insecurity of the letters in his
keeping. Swift ignored the request, and his letters about
this time began to show that his memory was failing and
his intellect growing weak.

[3] These expressions come from two letters of Pope to Lord
Orrery in March, 1737, and may not accurately reproduce his
statements to Swift; but they probably represent approximately
what he had said.

Pope now applied to their common friend Lord Orrery.
Orrery was the dull member of a family eminent for its
talents. His father had left a valuable library to Christ
Church, ostensibly because the son was not capable of
profiting by books, though a less creditable reason has
been assigned.[4] The son, eager to wipe off the imputation, specially affected the society of wits, and was elaborately polite both to Swift and Pope. Pope now got
Orrery to intercede with Swift, urging that the letters
were no longer safe in the custody of a failing old man.
Orrery succeeded, and brought the letters in a sealed
packet to Pope in the summer of 1737. Swift, it must
be added, had an impression that there was a gap of six
years in the collection ; he became confused as to what
had or had not been sent, and had a vague belief in a
"great collection" of letters "placed in some very safe
hand."[5] Pope, being thus in possession of the whole
correspondence, proceeded to perform a manœuvre resembling those already employed in the case of the
Dunciad and of the P. T. letters. He printed the
correspondence clandestinely. He then sent the printed
volume to Swift, accompanied by an anonymous letter.
This letter purported to come from some persons
who, from admiration of Swift's private and public
virtues, had resolved to preserve letters so creditable to him, and had accordingly put them in type.
They suggested that the volume would be suppressed if it
fell into the hands of Bolingbroke and Pope (a most
audacious suggestion !), and intimated that Swift should
himself publish it. No other copy, they said, was in exis-

[4] It is said that the son objected to allow his wife to meet his
father's mistress.

[5] See Elwin's edition of Pope's Correspondence, iii., 399, note.

tence.   Poor Swift fell at once into the trap.   He ought,
of course, to have consulted Pope or Bolingbroke, and
would probably have done so had his mind been sound.
Seeing, however, a volume already printed, he might
naturally suppose that, in spite of the anonymous as-
surance, it was already too late to stop the publication.   At any rate, he at once sent it to his publisher,
Faulkner, and desired him to bring it out at once.
Swift was in that most melancholy state in which a
man's friends perceive him to be incompetent to manage
his affairs, and are yet not able to use actual restraint.
Mrs. Whiteway, the sensible and affectionate cousin who
took care of him at this time, did her best to protest
against the publication, but in vain.   Swift insisted.   So
far Pope's device was successful.   The printed letters
had been placed in the hands of his bookseller by Swift
himself, and publication was apparently secured.   But
Pope had still the same problem as in the previous case.
Though he had talked of erecting a monument to Swift
and himself, he was anxious that the monument should
apparently be erected by some one else.   His vanity
could only be satisfied by the appearance that the publication was forced upon him.   He had, therefore, to dis-
sociate himself from the publication by some protest at
once emphatic and ineffectual ; and, consequently, to explain the means by which the letters had been surrep-
titiously obtained.

   The first aim was unexpectedly difficult.   Faulkner
turned out to be an honest bookseller.   Instead of sharing
Curll's rapacity, he consented, at Mrs. Whiteway's request,
to wait until Pope had an opportunity of expressing his
wishes.   Pope, if he consented, could no longer complain ; if he dissented, Faulkner would suppress the

letters. In this dilemma, Pope first wrote to Faulkner to refuse permission, and at the same time took care that his letter should be delayed for a month. He hoped that Faulkner would lose patience, and publish. But Faulkner, with provoking civility, stopped the press as soon as he heard of Pope's objection. Pope hereupon discovered that the letters were certain to be published, as they were already printed, and doubtless by some mysterious "confederacy of people" in London. All he could wish was to revise them before appearance. Meanwhile he begged Lord Orrery to inspect the book, and say what he thought of it. "Guess in what a situation I must be," exclaimed this sincere and modest person, "not to be able to see what all the world is to read as mine !" Orrery was quite as provoking as Faulkner. He got the book from Faulkner, read it, and instead of begging Pope not to deprive the world of so delightful a treat, said with dull integrity, that he thought the collection "unworthy to be published." Orrery, however, was innocent enough to accept Pope's suggestion, that letters which had once got into such hands would certainly come out sooner or later. After some more haggling, Pope ultimately decided to take this ground. He would, he said, have nothing to do with the letters ; they would come out in any case ; their appearance would please the Dean, and he (Pope) would stand clear of all responsibility. He tried, indeed, to get Faulkner to prefix a statement tending to fix the whole transaction upon Swift ; but the bookseller declined, and the letters ultimately came out with a simple statement that they were a reprint.

Pope had thus virtually sanctioned the publication. He was not the less emphatic in complaining of it to his friends. To Orrery, who knew the facts, he represented

the printed copy sent to Swift as a proof that the letters
were beyond his power ; and to others, such as his friend
Allen, he kept silence as to this copy altogether ; and gave
them to understand that poor Swift—or some member of
Swift's family—was the prime mover in the business.
His mystification had, as before, driven him into perplexities upon which he had never calculated.   In fact,
it was still more difficult here than in the previous case
to account for the original misappropriation of the letters.
Who could the thief have been?   Orrery, as we have
seen, had himself taken a packet of letters to Pope, which
would be of course the letters from Pope to Swift.   The
packet being sealed, Orrery did not know the contents,
and Pope asserted that he had burnt it almost as soon as
received.   It was, however, true that Swift had been in
the habit of showing the originals to his friends, and
some might possibly have been stolen or copied by
designing people.   But this would not account for the
publication of Swift's letters to Pope, which had never
been out of Pope's possession.   As he had certainly been
in possession of the other letters, it was easiest, even for
himself, to suppose that some of his own servants were
the guilty persons ; his own honour being, of course,
beyond question.

To meet these difficulties, Pope made great use of some
stray phrases dropped by Swift in the decline of his
memory, and set up a story of his having himself returned
some letters to Swift, of which important fact all traces
had disappeared.   One characteristic device will be a
sufficient specimen.   Swift wrote that a great collection
of "*my* letters to *you*" is somewhere "in a safe hand."
He meant, of course, "a collection of *your* letters to *me*"—
the only letters of which he could know anything.   Ob-

serving the slip of the pen, he altered the phrase by writing the correct words above the line. It now stood— "$\frac{your}{my}$ letters to $\frac{me}{you}$." Pope laid great stress upon this, interpreting it to mean that the "great collection" included letters from each correspondent to the other—the fact being that Swift had only the letters from Pope to himself. The omission of an erasure (whether by Swift or Pope) caused the whole meaning to be altered. As the great difficulty was to explain the publication of Swift's letters to Pope, this change supplied a very important link in the evidence. It implied that Swift had been at some time in possession of the letters in question, and had trusted them to some one supposed to be safe. The whole paragraph, meanwhile, appears, from the unimpeachable evidence of Mrs. Whiteway, to have involved one of the illusions of memory, for which he (Swift) apologizes in the letter from which this is extracted. By insisting upon this passage, and upon certain other letters dexterously confounded with those published, Pope succeeded in raising dust enough to blind Lord Orrery's not very piercing intelligence. The inference which he desired to suggest was that some persons in Swift's family had obtained possession of the letters. Mrs. Whiteway, indeed, met the suggestion so clearly, and gave such good reasons for assigning Twickenham as the probable centre of the plot, that she must have suspected the truth. Pope did not venture to assail her publicly, though he continued to talk of treachery or evil influence.

To accuse innocent people of a crime which you know yourself to have committed is bad enough. It is, perhaps, even baser to lay a trap for a friend, and reproach him for falling into it. Swift had denied the publication of the letters, and Pope would have had some grounds of complaint had he not been aware of the failure of Swift's mind, and had he not been himself the tempter. His position, however, forced him to blame his friend. It was a necessary part of his case to impute at least a breach of confidence to his victim. He therefore took the attitude—it must, one hopes, have cost him a blush— of one who is seriously aggrieved, but who is generously anxious to shield a friend in consideration of his known infirmity. He is forced, in sorrow, to admit that Swift has erred, but he will not allow himself to be annoyed. The most humiliating words ever written by a man not utterly vile, must have been those which Pope set down in a letter to Nugent, after giving his own version of the case: "I think I can make no reflections upon this strange incident but what are truly melancholy, and humble the pride of human nature. That the greatest of geniuses, though prudence may have been the companion of wit (which is very rare) for their whole lives past, may have nothing left them but their vanity. No decay of body is half so miserable." The most auda- cious hypocrite of fiction pales beside this. Pope, con- descending to the meanest complication of lies to justify a paltry vanity, taking advantage of his old friend's dotage to trick him into complicity, then giving a false account of his error, and finally moralizing, with all the airs of philosophic charity, and taking credit for his gene- rosity, is altogether a picture to set fiction at defiance.

I must add a remark not so edifying. Pope went down to his grave soon afterwards, without exciting sus- picion except among two or three people intimately concerned. A whisper of doubt was soon hushed. Even the biographers who were on the track of his former deception did not suspect this similar iniquity. The last of them, Mr. Carruthers, writing in 1857, observes upon the pain given to Pope by the treachery of Swift— a treachery of course palliated by Swift's failure of mind. At last Mr. Dilke discovered the truth, which has been placed beyond doubt by the still later discovery of the letters to Orrery. The moral is, apparently, that it is better to cheat a respectable man than a rogue; for the respectable tacitly form a society for mutual support of character, whilst the open rogue will be only too glad to show that you are even such an one as himself.

It was not probable that letters thus published should be printed with scrupulous accuracy. Pope, indeed, can scarcely have attempted to conceal the fact that they had been a good deal altered. And so long as the letters were regarded merely as literary compositions, the practice was at least pardonable. But Pope went further; and the full extent of his audacious changes was not seen until Mr. Dilke became possessed of the Caryll correspondence. On comparing the copies preserved by Caryll with the letters published by Pope, it became evident that Pope had regarded these letters as so much raw material, which he might carve into shape at pleasure, and with such alterations of date and address as might be convenient, to the confusion of all biographers and editors ignorant of his peculiar method of editing. The details of these very disgraceful falsifications have been fully described by Mr. Elwin,[6] but I turn gladly from this lamentable narrative to say something of the literary value of the correspondence. Every critic has made the obvious remark that Pope's letters are artificial and self-conscious. Pope claimed the opposite merit. " It is many years," he says to Swift in

[6] Pope's Works, vol. i. p. cxxi.

1734, "since I wrote as a wit." He smiles to think
"how Curll would be bit were our epistles to fall into
his hands, and how gloriously they would fall short of
every ingenious reader's anticipations." Warburton adds
in a note that Pope used to "value himself upon this
particular." It is indeed true that Pope had dropped the
boyish affectation of his letters to Wycherley and Cromwell. But such a statement in the mouth of a man who
plotted to secure Curll's publication of his letters, with
devices elaborate enough to make the reputation of an
unscrupulous diplomatist, is of course only one more
example of the superlative degree of affectation, the affectation of being unaffected. We should be indeed disappointed were we to expect in Pope's letters what we
find in the best specimens of the art : the charm which
belongs to a simple outpouring of friendly feeling in
private intercourse ; the sweet playfulness of Cowper, or
the grave humour of Gray, or even the sparkle and brilliance of Walpole's admirable letters. Though Walpole
had an eye to posterity, and has his own mode of affectation, he is for the moment intent on amusing, and is free
from the most annoying blemish in Pope's writing, the
resolution to appear always in full dress, and to mount as
often as possible upon the stilts of moral self-approbation.
All this is obvious to the hasty reader ; and yet I must
confess my own conviction that there is scarcely a more
interesting volume in the language than that which contains the correspondence of Swift, Bolingbroke, and Pope.
To enjoy it, indeed, we must not expect to be in sympathy with the writers. Rather we must adopt the mental
attitude of spectators of a scene of high comedy—the
comedy which is dashed with satire and has a tragical
side to it. We are behind the scenes in Vanity Fair, and
listening to the talk of three of its most famous per-

formers, doubting whether they most deceive each other
or the public or themselves. The secret is an open one
for us, now that the illusion which perplexed contemporaries has worn itself threadbare.

The most impressive letters are undoubtedly those of
Swift—the stern sad humourist, frowning upon the world
which has rejected him, and covering his wrath with an
affectation, not of fine sentiment, but of misanthropy. A
soured man prefers to turn his worst side outwards. There
are phrases in his letters which brand themselves upon
the memory like those of no other man ; and we are
softened into pity as the strong mind is seen gradually
sinking into decay. The two other sharers in the colloquy
are in effective contrast. We see through Bolingbroke's
magnificent self-deceit ; the flowing manners of the statesman who, though the game is lost, is longing for a favour-
able turn of the card, but still affects to solace himself
with philosophy, and wraps himself in dignified reflections
upon the blessings of retirement, contrast with Swift's
downright avowal of indignant scorn for himself and mankind. And yet we have a sense of the man's amazing
cleverness, and regret that he has no chance of trying one
more fall with his antagonists in the open arena. Pope's
affectation is perhaps the most transparent and the most
gratuitous. His career had been pre-eminently successful ;
his talents had found their natural outlet ; and he had
only to be what he apparently persuaded himself that he
was, to be happy in spite of illness. He is constantly
flourishing his admirable moral sense in our faces, dilating
upon his simplicity, modesty, fidelity to his friends, indifference to the charms of fame, till we are almost convinced that he has imposed upon himself. By some
strange piece of legerdemain he must surely have succeeded in regarding even his deliberate artifices, with

the astonishing masses of hypocritical falsehoods which
they entailed, as in some way legitimate weapons against
a world full of piratical Curlls and deep laid plots. And,
indeed, with all his delinquencies, and with all his affecta-
tions, there are moments in which we forget to preserve
the correct tone of moral indignation. Every now and
then genuine feeling seems to come to the surface. For
a time the superincumbent masses of hypocrisy vanish.
In speaking of his mother or his pursuits he forgets to wear
his mask. He feels a genuine enthusiasm about his
friends ; he believes with almost pathetic earnestness in the
amazing talents of Bolingbroke, and the patriotic devotion
of the younger men who are rising up to overthrow the
corruptions of Walpole ; he takes the affectation of his
friends as seriously as a simple-minded man who has never
fairly realized the possibility of deliberate hypocrisy ; and
he utters sentiments about human life and its objects
which, if a little tainted with commonplace, have yet a
certain ring of sincerity and, as we may believe, were
really sincere for the time. At such moments we seem to
see the man behind the veil—the really loveable nature
which could know as well as simulate feeling. And, indeed,
it is this quality which makes Pope endurable. He was—
if we must speak bluntly—a liar and a hypocrite ; but
the foundation of his character was not selfish or grovelling.
On the contrary, no man could be more warmly affectionate or more exquisitely sensitive to many noble
emotions. The misfortune was that his constitutional
infirmities, acted upon by unfavourable conditions, deve-
loped his craving for applause and his fear of censure, till
certain morbid tendencies in him assumed proportions
which, compared to the same weaknesses in ordinary mankind, are as the growth of plants in a tropical forest to
their stunted representatives in the North.

CHAPTER VII.

THE ESSAY ON MAN.

It is a relief to turn from this miserable record of Pope's petty or malicious deceptions to the history of his legitimate career. I go back to the period when he was still in full power. Having finished the Dunciad, he was soon employed on a more ambitious task. Pope resembled one of the inferior bodies of the solar system, whose orbit is dependent upon that of some more massive planet ; and having been a satellite of Swift, he was now swept into the train of the more imposing Bolingbroke. He had been originally introduced to Bolingbroke by Swift, but had probably seen little of the brilliant minister who, in the first years of their acquaintance, had too many occupations to give much time to the rising poet. Bolingbroke, however, had been suffering a long eclipse, whilst Pope was gathering fresh splendour. In his exile, Bolingbroke, though never really weaned from political ambition, had amused himself with superficial philosophical studies. In political life it was his special glory to extemporize statesmanship without sacrificing pleasure. He could be at once the most reckless of rakes and the leading spirit in the Cabinet or the House of Commons. He seems to have thought that philosophical eminence was obtainable in the same offhand fashion, and that a brilliant style

would justify a man in laying down the law to meta-
physicians as well as to diplomatists and politicians. His
philosophical writings are equally superficial and arrogant,
though they show here and there the practised debater's
power of making a good point against his antagonist
without really grasping the real problems at issue.

Bolingbroke received a pardon in 1723, and returned to
England, crossing Atterbury, who had just been convicted
of treasonable practices. In 1725 Bolingbroke settled at
Dawley, near Uxbridge, and for the next ten years he was
alternately amusing himself in playing the retired philosopher, and endeavouring, with more serious purpose, to
animate the opposition to Walpole. Pope, who was his
frequent guest, sympathized with his schemes, and was
completely dazzled by his eminence. He spoke of him
with bated breath, as a being almost superior to humanity.
"It looks," said Pope once, "as if that great man had
been placed here by mistake. When the comet appeared
a month or two ago," he added, "I sometimes fancied
that it might be come to carry him home, as a coach comes
to one's door for other visitors." Of all the graceful compliments in Pope's poetry, none are more ardent or more
obviously sincere than those addressed to this "guide,
philosopher, and friend." He delighted to bask in the
sunshine of the great man's presence. Writing to Swift
in 1728, he (Pope) says that he is holding the pen "for
my Lord Bolingbroke," who is reading your letter between
two haycocks, with his attention occasionally distracted
by a threatening shower. Bolingbroke is acting the temperate recluse, having nothing for dinner but mutton-
broth, beans and bacon, and a barndoor fowl. Whilst
his lordship is running after a cart, Pope snatches a
moment to tell how the day before this noble farmer had

engaged a painter for 200*l.* to give the correct agricultural
air to his country hall by ornamenting it with trophies of
spades, rakes, and prongs.   Pope saw that the zeal for
retirement was not free from affectation, but he sat at the
teacher's feet with profound belief in the value of the
lessons which flowed from his lips.

The connexion was to bear remarkable fruit.   Under
the direction of Bolingbroke, Pope resolved to compose a
great philosophical poem.   "Does Pope talk to you," says
Bolingbroke to Swift in 1731, " of the noble work which,
at my instigation, he has begun in such a manner that he
must be convinced by this time I judged better of his
talents than he did?"   And Bolingbroke proceeds to
describe the Essay on Man, of which it seems that three
(out of four) epistles were now finished.   The first of these
epistles appeared in 1733.   Pope, being apparently nervous
on his first appearance as a philosopher, withheld his
name.   The other parts followed in the course of 1733
and 1734, and the authorship was soon avowed.   The
Essay on Man is Pope's most ambitious performance,
and the one by which he was best known beyond his own
country.   It has been frequently translated, it was imitated both in France and Germany, and provoked a controversy, not like others in Pope's history of the purely
personal kind.

The Essay on Man professes to be a theodicy.   Pope,
with an echo of the Miltonic phrase, proposes to

> Vindicate the ways of God to man.

He is thus attempting the greatest task to which poet
or philosopher can devote himself—the exhibition of an
organic and harmonious view of the universe.   In a time
when men's minds are dominated by a definite religious

creed, the poet may hope to achieve success in such an undertaking without departing from his legitimate method. His vision pierces to the world hidden from our senses, and realizes in the transitory present a scene in the slow development of a divine drama. To make us share his vision is to give his justification of Providence. When Milton told the story of the war in heaven and the fall of man, he gave implicitly his theory of the true relations of man to his Creator, but the abstract doctrine was clothed in the flesh and blood of a concrete mythology.

In Pope's day the traditional belief had lost its hold upon men's minds too completely to be used for imaginative purposes. The story of Adam and Eve would itself require to be justified or to be rationalized into thin allegory. Nothing was left possessed of any vitality but a bare skeleton of abstract theology, dependent upon argument instead of tradition, and which might use or might dispense with a Christian phraseology. Its deity was not a historical personage, but the name of a metaphysical conception. For a revelation was substituted a demonstration. To vindicate Providence meant no longer to stimulate imagination by pure and sublime rendering of accepted truths, but to solve certain philosophical problems, and especially the grand difficulty of reconciling the existence of evil with divine omnipotence and benevolence.

Pope might conceivably have written a really great poem on these terms, though deprived of the concrete imagery of a Dante or a Milton. If he had fairly grasped some definite conception of the universe, whether pantheistic or atheistic, optimist or pessimist, proclaiming a solution of the mystery, or declaring all solutions to be impossible, he might have given forcible expression to the

corresponding emotions. Hè might have uttered the melancholy resignation and the confident hope incited in different minds by a contemplation of the mysterious world.
He might again conceivably have written an interesting
work, though it would hardly have been a poem—if he had
versified the arguments by which a coherent theory might
be supported. Unluckily, he was quite unqualified for either
undertaking, and, at the same time, he more or less aimed
at both. Anything like sustained reasoning was beyond
his reach. Pope felt and thought by shocks and electric
flashes. He could only obtain a continuous effect when
working clearly upon lines already provided for him, or
simulate one by fitting together fragments struck out at
intervals. The defect was aggravated or caused by the
physical infirmities which put sustained intellectual labour
out of the question. The laborious and patient meditation
which brings a converging series of arguments to bear
upon a single point, was to him as impossible as the power
of devising an elaborate strategical combination to a dash-
ing Prince Rupert. The reasonings in the Essay are confused, contradictory, and often childish. He was equally
far from having assimilated any definite system of thought.
Brought up as a Catholic, he had gradually swung into
vague deistic belief. But he had never studied any philosophy or theology whatever, and he accepts in perfect unconsciousness fragments of the most heterogeneous systems.

Swift, in verses from which I have already quoted,
describes his method of composition, which is characteristic
of Pope's habits of work.

> Now backs of letters, though design'd
> For those who more will need 'em,
> Are fill'd with hints and interlined,
> Himself can scarcely read 'em.

Each atom by some other struck
All turns and motions tries ;
Till in a lump together stuck
Behold a poem rise !

It was strange enough that any poem should arise by
such means ; but it would have been miraculous if a poem
so constructed had been at once a demonstration and an
exposition of a harmonious philosophical system. The
confession which he made to Warburton will be a sufficient indication of his qualifications as a student. He
says (in 1739) that he never in his life read a line of
Leibnitz, nor knew, till he found it in a confutation of his
Essay, that there was such a term as pre-established harmony. That is almost as if a modern reconciler of faith
and science were to say that he had never read a line of
Mr. Darwin, or heard of such a phrase as the struggle for
existence. It was to pronounce himself absolutely disqualified to speak as a philosopher.

How, then, could Pope obtain even an appearance of
success ? The problem should puzzle no one at the present
day. Every smart essayist knows how to settle the most
abstruse metaphysical puzzles after studies limited to the
pages of a monthly magazine ; and Pope was much in
the state of mind of such extemporizing philosophers.
He had dipped into the books which everybody read ;
Locke's Essay, and Shaftesbury's Characteristics, and
Wollaston's Religion of Nature, and Clarke on the
Attributes, and Archbishop King on the Origin of Evil,
had probably amused his spare moments. They were
all, we may suppose, in Bolingbroke's library ; and if that
passing shower commemorated in Pope's letter drove them
back to the house, Bolingbroke might discourse from the
page which happened to be open, and Pope would try to

versify it on the back of an envelope.[7] Nor must we forget, like some of his commentators, that after all Pope was an exceedingly clever man. His rapidly perceptive mind was fully qualified to imbibe the crude versions of philosophic theories which float upon the surface of ordinary talk, and are not always so inferior to their prototypes in philosophic qualities, as philosophers would have us believe. He could by snatches seize with admirable quickness the general spirit of a doctrine, though unable to sustain himself at a high intellectual level for any length of time. He was ready with abundance of poetical illustrations, not, perhaps, very closely adapted to the logic, but capable of being elaborated into effective passages ; and, finally, Pope had always a certain number of more or less appropriate commonplaces or renderings into verse of some passages which had struck him in Pascal, or Rochefoucauld, or Bacon, all of them favourite authors, and which could be wrought into the structure at a slight cost of coherence. By such means he could put together a poem, which was certainly not an organic whole, but which might contain many striking sayings and passages of great rhetorical effect.

The logical framework was, we may guess, supplied mainly by Bolingbroke. Bathurst told Warton that Bolingbroke had given Pope the essay in prose, and that Pope had only turned it into verse ; and Mallet—a friend of both— is said to have seen the very manuscript from which Pope worked. Johnson, on hearing this from Boswell, remarked that it must be an overstatement. Pope might have had from Bolingbroke the "philosophical stamina" of the essay, but he must, at least, have contributed the "poetical ima-

[7] "No letter with an envelope could give him more delight," says Swift.

gery," and have had more independent power than the
story implied.　It is, indeed, impossible accurately to fix
the relations of the teacher and his disciple.　Pope acknowledged in the strongest possible terms his dependence upon
Bolingbroke, and Bolingbroke claims with equal dis-
tinctness the position of instigator and inspirer.　His
more elaborate philosophical works are in the form of
letters to Pope, and profess to be a redaction of the con-
versations which they had had together.　These were not
written till after the Essay on Man ; but a series of fragments appear to represent what he actually set down for
Pope's guidance.　They are professedly addressed to Pope.
" I write," he says (fragment 65), " to you and for you,
and you would think yourself little obliged to me if I
took the pains of explaining in prose what you would not
think it necessary to explain in verse,"—that is, the free-
will puzzle.　The manuscripts seen by Mallet may probable have been a commonplace book in which Bolingbroke had set down some of these fragments, by way of
instructing Pope, and preparing for his own more systematic
work.　No reader of the fragments can, I think, doubt as
to the immediate source of Pope's inspiration.　Most of
the ideas expressed were the common property of many
contemporary writers, but Pope accepts the particular modification presented by Bolingbroke.[8]　Pope's manipulation
of these materials causes much of the Essay on Man
to resemble (as Mr. Pattison puts it) an exquisite mosaic
work.　A detailed examination of his mode of transmu-
tation would be a curious study in the technical secrets of

[8] It would be out of place to discuss this in detail; but I may
say that Pope's crude theory of the state of nature, his psychology
as to reason and instinct, and self-love, and his doctrine of the
scale of beings, all seem to have the specific Bolingbroke stamp.

literary execution. A specimen or two will sufficiently
indicate the general character of Pope's method of con-
structing his essay.

The forty-third fragment of Bolingbroke is virtually a
prose version of much of Pope's poetry. A few phrases
will exhibit the relation :—

> Through worlds unnumber'd though the God be known,
> 'Tis ours to *trace Him only in our own.*
> He who through vast immensity can pierce,
> See worlds on worlds *compose one universe,*
> Observe how *system into system runs,*
> What other planets circle other suns,
> What varied being peoples every star,
> May tell why Heaven has made us what we are.
> But of this frame the bearings and *the ties,*
> The strong *connexions,* nice *dependencies,*
> *Gradations* just, has thy pervading soul
> Looked through, or can a part contain the whole ?

"The universe," I quote only a few phrases from
Bolingbroke, "is an immense aggregate of systems.
Every one of these, *if we may judge by our own,* contains
several, and every one of these again, *if we may judge by our
own,* is made up of a multitude of different modes of being,
animated and inanimated, thinking and unthinking . . .
but all concurring in one common system. . . . Just
so it is with respect to the various systems and *systems of
systems that compose the universe.* As distant as they
are, and as different as we may imagine them to be, they
are all *tied* together by relations and *connexions, grada-
tions,* and *dependencies.*" The verbal coincidence is here
as marked as the coincidence in argument. Warton
refers to an eloquent passage in Shaftesbury, which contains a similar thought ; but one can hardly doubt that
Bolingbroke was in this case the immediate source. A

quaint passage a little farther on, in which Pope represents man as complaining because he has not "the
strength of bulls or the fur of bears," may be traced with
equal plausibility to Shaftesbury or to Sir Thomas
Browne; but I have not noticed it in Bolingbroke.

One more passage will be sufficient. Pope asks whether
we are to demand the suspension of laws of nature whenever they might produce a mischievous result? Is Etna
to cease an eruption to spare a sage, or should "new
motions be impressed upon sea and air" for the advantage of blameless Bethel?

> When the loose mountain trembles from on high
> Shall gravitation cease, if you go by?
> Or some old temple, nodding to its fall,
> For Chartres' head reserve the hanging wall?

Chartres is Pope's typical villain. This is a terse version, with concrete cases, of Bolingbroke's vaguer gene-
ralities. "The laws of gravitation," he says, "must
sometimes be suspended (if special Providence be admitted), and sometimes their effect must be precipitated.
The tottering edifice must be kept miraculously from falling, whilst innocent men lived in it or passed under it,
and the fall of it must be as miraculously determined to
crush the guilty inhabitant or passenger." Here, again,
we have the alternative of Wollaston, who uses a similar
illustration, and in one phrase comes nearer to Pope. He
speaks of "new motions being impressed upon the atmosphere." We may suppose that the two friends had been
dipping into Wollaston together. Elsewhere Pope seems
to have stolen for himself. In the beginning of the
second epistle, Pope, in describing man as "the glory,
jest, and riddle of the world," is simply versifying Pascal;
and a little farther on, when he speaks of reason as the

wind and passion as the gale on life's vast ocean, he is adapting his comparison from Locke's treatise on government.

If all such cases were adduced, we should have nearly picked the argumentative part of the essay to pieces; but Bolingbroke supplies throughout the most characteristic element. The fragments cohere by external cement, not by an internal unity of thought; and Pope too often descends to the level of mere satire, or indulges in a quaint conceit or palpable sophistry. Yet it would be very unjust to ignore the high qualities which are to be found in this incongruous whole. The style is often admirable. When Pope is at his best every word tells. His precision and firmness of touch enables him to get the greatest possible meaning into a narrow compass. He uses only one epithet, but it is the right one, and never boggles and patches or, in his own phrase, " blunders round about a meaning." Warton gives, as a specimen of this power, the lines :—

> But errs not nature from this gracious end
> From burning suns when livid deaths descend,
> When earthquakes swallow or when tempests sweep
> Towns to one grave, whole nations to the deep ?

And Mr. Pattison reinforces the criticism by quoting Voltaire's feeble imitation :—

> Quand des vents du midi les funestes haleines
> De semence de mort ont inondé nos plaines,
> Direz-vous que jamais le ciel en son courroux
> Ne laissa la santé séjourner parmi nous ?

It is true that in the effort to be compressed, Pope has here and there cut to the quick and suppressed essential parts of speech, till the lines can only be construed by our

independent knowledge of their meaning. The famous
line—

Man never is but always to be blest,

is an example of defective construction, though his language is often tortured by more elliptical phrases.[9] This
power of charging lines with great fulness of meaning
enables Pope to soar for brief periods into genuine and
impressive poetry. Whatever his philosophical weakness
and his moral obliquity, he is often moved by genuine
emotion. He has a vein of generous sympathy for human
sufferings and of righteous indignation against bigots,
and if he only half understands his own optimism, that
"whatever is is right," the vision, rather poetical than
philosophical, of a harmonious universe lifts him at times
into a region loftier than that of frigid and pedantic
platitude. The most popular passages were certain purple
patches, not arising very spontaneously or with much
relevance, but also showing something more than the
practised rhetorician. The "poor Indian" in one of the
most highly-polished paragraphs—

Who thinks, admitted to that equal sky,
His faithful dog shall bear him company,

intrudes rather at the expense of logic, and is a decidedly
conventional person. But this passage has a certain glow of
fine humanity and is touched with real pathos. A further

---

[9] Perhaps the most curious example, too long for quotation, is a
passage near the end of the last epistle, in which he sums up his
moral system by a series of predicates for which it is impossible
to find any subject. One couplet runs—

Never elated whilst one man's depress'd,
Never dejected whilst another's blest.

It is impressive, but it is quite impossible to discover by the rules of
grammatical construction who is to be never elated and depressed.

passage or two may sufficiently indicate his higher qualities.
In the end of the third epistle Pope is discussing the
origin of government and the state of nature, and discussing them in such a way as to show conclusively that he
does not in the least understand the theories in question
or their application. His state of Nature is a sham reproduction of the golden age of poets, made to do
duty in a scientific speculation. A flimsy hypothesis
learnt from Bolingbroke is not improved when overlaid
with Pope's conventional ornamentation. The imaginary
history proceeds to relate the growth of superstition,
which destroys the primeval innocence ; but why or when
does not very clearly appear ; yet, though the general
theory is incoherent, he catches a distinct view of one
aspect of the question and expresses a tolerably trite view
of the question with singular terseness. Who, he asks, —

> First taught souls enslaved and realms undone,
> The enormous faith of many made for one ?

He replies,—

> Force first made conquest and that conquest law ;
> Till Superstition taught the tyrant awe,
> Then shared the tyranny, then lent it aid,
> And gods of conquerors, slaves of subjects made ;
> She, 'mid the lightning's blaze and thunder's sound,
> When rock'd the mountains and when groan'd the ground—
> She taught the weak to trust, the proud to pray
> To Power unseen and mightier far than they ;
> She from the rending earth and bursting skies
> Saw gods descend and fiends infernal rise ;
> There fix'd the dreadful, there the blest abodes ;
> Fear made her devils, and weak hope her gods ;
> Gods partial, changeful, passionate, unjust,
> Whose attributes were rage, revenge, or lust ;
> Such as the souls of cowards might conceive,
> And, framed like tyrants, tyrants would believe.

If the test of poetry were the power of expressing a
theory more closely and pointedly than prose, such writing
would take a very high place. Some popular philosophers
would make a sounding chapter out of those sixteen lines.

The Essay on Man brought Pope into difficulties. The
central thesis, " whatever is is right," might be understood in various senses, and in some sense it would be
accepted by every theist. But, in Bolingbroke's teaching,
it received a heterodox application, and in Pope's imperfect version of Bolingbroke the taint was not removed.
The logical outcome of the rationalistic theory of the
time was some form of pantheism, and the tendency is
still more marked in a poetical statement, where it was
difficult to state the refined distinctions by which the
conclusion is averted. When theology is regarded as de-
monstrable by reason, the need of a revelation ceases to be
obvious. The optimistic view which sees the proof of
divine order in the vast harmony of the whole visible
world, throws into the background the darker side of the
universe reflected in the theological doctrines of human
corruption, and the consequent need of a future judgment
in separation of good from evil. I need not inquire
whether any optimistic theory is really tenable ; but the
popular version of the creed involved the attempt to
ignore the evils under which all creation groans, and
produced in different minds the powerful retort of Butler's
Analogy, and the biting sarcasm of Voltaire's Can-
dide. Pope, accepting the doctrine without any perception of these difficulties, unintentionally fell into
sheer pantheism. He was not yielding to the logical
instinct which carries out a theory to its legitimate
development ; but obeying the imaginative impulse which
cannot stop to listen to the usual qualifications and safe-

guards of the orthodox reasoner.   The best passages in
the essay are those in which he is frankly pantheistic,
and is swept, like Shaftesbury, into enthusiastic assertion
of the universal harmony of things.

> All are but parts of one stupendous whole,
> Whose body nature is, and God the soul;
> That changed thro' all and yet in all the same,
> Great in the earth as in the ethereal frame ;
> Warms in the sun, refreshes in the breeze,
> Glows in the stars, and blossoms in the trees ;
> Lives thro' all life, extends thro' all extent,
> Spreads undivided, operates unspent ;
> Breathes in our soul, informs our mortal part,
> As full, as perfect, in a hair as heart ;
> As full, as perfect, in vile man that mourns,
> As the rapt seraph that adores and burns ;
> To him, no high, no low, no great, no small,
> He fills, he bounds, connects, and equals all.

In spite of some awkward phrases (hair and heart is a
vile antithesis !), the passage is eloquent but can hardly be
called orthodox.   And it was still worse when Pope undertook to show that even evil passions and vices were part of
the harmony ; that " a Borgia and a Cataline " were as much
a part of the divine order as a plague or an earthquake,
and that self-love and lust were essential to social welfare.

Pope's own religious position is characteristic and easily
definable.   If it is not quite defensible on the strictest
principles of plain speaking, it is also certain that we
could not condemn him without condemning many of the
best and most catholic-spirited of men.   The dogmatic
system in which he had presumably been educated had
softened under the influence of the cultivated thought of
the day.   Pope, as the member of a persecuted sect, had
learnt to share that righteous hatred of bigotry which is
the honourable characteristic of his best contemporaries.

He considered the persecuting spirit of his own church to
be its worst fault.[1]   In the early Essay on Criticism he
offended some of his own sect by a vigorous denunciation
of the doctrine which promotes persecution by limiting
salvation to a particular creed.   His charitable conviction
that a divine element is to be found in all creeds, from
that of the "poor Indian" upwards, animates the highest
passages in his works.   But though he sympathizes
with a generous toleration, and the specific dogmas of his
creed sat very loosely on his mind, he did not consider
that an open secession was necessary or even honourable.
He called himself a true Catholic, though rather as respect-
fully sympathizing with the spirit of Fénelon than as
holding to any dogmatic system.   The most dignified
letter that he ever wrote was in answer to a suggestion
from Atterbury (1717), that he might change his religion
upon the death of his father.   Pope replies that his
worldly interests would be promoted by such a step ; and,
in fact, it cannot be doubted that Pope might have had a
share in the good things then obtainable by successful
writers, if he had qualified by taking the oaths.   But he
adds, that such a change would hurt his mother's feelings,
and that he was more certain of his duty to promote her
happiness than of any speculative tenet whatever.   He
was sure that he could mean as well in the religion he
now professed as in any other ; and that being so, he
thought that a change even to an equally good religion
could not be justified.   A similar statement appears in a
letter to Swift, in 1729.   " I am of the religion of Erasmus, a Catholic.   So I live, so shall I die, and hope one
day to meet you, Bishop Atterbury, the younger Craggs,
Dr. Garth, Dean Berkeley, and Mr. Hutchison in that

[1] Spence, p. 364.

place to which God of his infinite mercy bring us and everybody." To these Protestants he would doubtless have joined the freethinking Bolingbroke. At a later period he told Warburton, in less elevated language, that the change of his creed would bring him many enemies and do no good to any one.

Pope could feel nobly and act honourably when his morbid vanity did not expose him to some temptation; and I think that in this matter his attitude was in every way creditable. He showed, indeed, the prejudice entertained by many of the rationalist divines for the freethinkers who were a little more outspoken than himself. The deist whose creed was varnished with Christian phrases, was often bitter against the deist who rejected the varnish; and Pope put Toland and Tindal into the Dunciad as scandalous assailants of all religion. From his point of view it was as wicked to attack any creed as to regard any creed as exclusively true; and certainly Pope was not disposed to join any party which was hated and maligned by the mass of the respectable world. For it must be remembered that, in spite of much that has been said to the contrary, and in spite of the true tendency of much so-called orthodoxy, the profession of open dissent from Christian doctrine was then regarded with extreme disapproval. It might be a fashion, as Butler and others declare, to talk infidelity in cultivated circles; but a public promulgation of unbelief was condemned as criminal, and worthy only of the Grub-street faction. Pope, therefore, was terribly shocked when he found himself accused of heterodoxy. His poem was at once translated, and, we are told, spread rapidly in France, where Voltaire and many inferior writers were introducing the contagion of English freethinking. A solid Swiss pastor

and professor of philosophy, Jean Pierre Crousaz (1663—
1750), undertook the task of refutation, and published an
examination of Pope's philosophy in 1737 and 1738.
A serious examination of this bundle of half-digested
opinions was in itself absurd. Some years afterwards
(1751) Pope came under a more powerful critic. The
Berlin Academy of Sciences offered a prize for a similar
essay, and Lessing published a short tract called *Pope ein
Metaphysiker!* If any one cares to see a demonstration
that Pope did not understand the system of Leibnitz, and
that the bubble blown by a great philosopher has more
apparent cohesion than that of a half-read poet, he may
find a sufficient statement of the case in Lessing. But
Lessing sensibly protests from the start against the intru-
sion of such a work into serious discussion; and that
is the only ground which is worth taking in the matter.

The most remarkable result of the Essay on Man,
it may be parenthetically noticed, was its effect upon
Voltaire. In 1751 Voltaire wrote a poem on Natural
Law, which is a comparatively feeble application of
Pope's principles. It is addressed to Frederick instead of
Bolingbroke, and contains a warm eulogy of Pope's
philosophy. But a few years later the earthquake at
Lisbon suggested certain doubts to Voltaire as to the
completeness of the optimist theory; and, in some of the
most impressive verses of the century, he issued an ener-
getic protest against the platitudes applied by Pope and
his followers to deaden our sense of the miseries under
which the race suffers. Verbally, indeed, Voltaire still
makes his bow to the optimist theory, and the two
poems appeared together in 1756; but his noble out-
cry against the empty and complacent deductions which
it covers, led to his famous controversy with Rousseau.

The history of this conflict falls beyond my subject, and
I must be content with this brief reference, which proves,
amongst other things, the interest created by Pope's advocacy of the most characteristic doctrines of his time on
the minds of the greatest leaders of the revolutionary
movement.

Meanwhile, however, Crousaz was translated into English, and Pope was terribly alarmed. His "guide, philosopher, and friend" had returned to the Continent (in
1735), disgusted with his political failure, but was again
in England from June, 1738, to May, 1739. We know
not what comfort he may have given to his unlucky disciple, but an unexpected champion suddenly arose.
William Warburton (born 1698) was gradually pushing
his way to success. He had been an attorney's clerk, and
had not received a university education; but his multifarious reading was making him conspicuous, helped by
great energy, and by a quality which gave some plausibility to the title bestowed on him by Mallet, "The
most impudent man living." In his humble days he had
been intimate with Pope's enemies, Concanen and Theobald, and had spoken scornfully of Pope, saying, amongst
other things, that he "borrowed for want of genius," as
Addison borrowed from modesty and Milton from pride.
In 1736 he had published his first important work, the
Alliance between Church and State, and in 1738 followed the first instalment of his principal performance,
the Divine Legation. During the following years he
was the most conspicuous theologian of the day, dreaded
and hated by his opponents, whom he unsparingly bullied,
and dominating a small clique of abject admirers. He is
said to have condemned the Essay on Man when it
first appeared. He called it a collection of the worst

N

passages of the worst authors, and declared that it
taught rank atheism.   The appearance of Crousaz's book
suddenly induced him to make a complete change of
front.   He declared that Pope spoke "truth uniformly
throughout," and complimented him on his strong and
delicate reasoning.

It is idle to seek motives for this proceeding.   Warburton loved paradoxes, and delighted in brandishing
them in the most offensive terms.   He enjoyed the exercise of his own ingenuity, and therefore his ponderous
writings, though amusing by their audacity and width
of reading, are absolutely valueless for their ostensible
purpose.   The exposition of Pope (the first part of which
appeared in December, 1738) is one of his most tiresome
performances ; nor need any human being at the present
day study the painful wire-drawings and sophistries by
which he tries to give logical cohesion and orthodox intention to the Essay on Man.

If Warburton was simply practising his dialectical skill,
the result was a failure.   But if he had an eye to certain
lower ends, his success surpassed his expectations.   Pope
was in ecstasies.   He fell upon Warburton's neck—or
rather at his feet—and overwhelmed him with professions
of gratitude.   He invited him to Twickenham ; met him
with compliments which astonished a bystander, and
wrote to him in terms of surprising humility.   "You
understand me," he exclaims in his first letter, "as well
as I do myself ; but you express me much better than
I could express myself."   For the rest of his life Pope
adopted the same tone.   He sheltered himself behind this
burly defender, and could never praise him enough.   He
declared Mr. Warburton to be the greatest general
critic he ever knew, and was glad to instal him in the

position of champion in ordinary. Warburton was consulted about new editions ; annotated Pope's poems ;
stood sponsor to the last Dunciad, and was assured by
his admiring friend that the comment would prolong the
life of the poetry. Pope left all his copyrights to this
friend, whilst his MSS. were given to Bolingbroke.

When the University of Oxford proposed to confer an
honorary degree upon Pope, he declined to receive the
compliment, because the proposal to confer a smaller
honour upon Warburton had been at the same time
thrown out by the University. In fact, Pope looked up
to Warburton with a reverence almost equal to that which
he felt for Bolingbroke. If such admiration for such an
idol was rather humiliating, we must remember that Pope
was unable to detect the charlatan in the pretentious but
really vigorous writer ; and we may perhaps admit that
there is something pathetic in Pope's constant eagerness
to be supported by some sturdier arm. We find the same
tendency throughout his life. The weak and morbidly
sensitive nature may be forgiven if its dependence leads
to excessive veneration.

Warburton derived advantages from the connexion, the
prospect of which, we may hope, was not the motive of
his first advocacy. To be recognized by the most eminent
man of letters of the day was to receive a kind of certifi-
cate of excellence, valuable to a man who had not the
regular university hall-mark. More definite results followed. Pope introduced Warburton to Allen, and to
Murray, afterwards Lord Mansfield. Through Murray
he was appointed preacher at Lincoln's Inn, and from
Allen he derived greater benefits—the hand of his niece
and heiress, and an introduction to Pitt, which gained for
him the bishopric of Gloucester.

Pope's allegiance to Bolingbroke was not weakened by this new alliance. He sought to bring the two together, when Bolingbroke again visited England in 1743. The only result was an angry explosion, as, indeed, might have been foreseen; for Bolingbroke was not likely to be well-disposed to the clever parson whose dexterous sleight-of-hand had transferred Pope to the orthodox camp; nor was it natural that Warburton, the most combative and insulting of controversialists, should talk on friendly terms to one of his natural antagonists—an antagonist, moreover, who was not likely to have bishoprics in his gift. The quarrel, as we shall see, broke out fiercely over Pope's grave.

CHAPTER VIII.

Pope had tried a considerable number of poetical experiments when the Dunciad appeared, but he had not yet discovered in what direction his talents could be most efficiently exerted. Bystanders are sometimes acuter in detecting a man's true forte than the performer himself. In 1722 Atterbury had seen Pope's lines upon Addison, and reported that no piece of his writing was ever so much sought after. "Since you now know," he added, "in what direction your strength lies, I hope you will not suffer that talent to be unemployed." Atterbury seems to have been rather fond of giving advice to Pope, and puts on a decidedly pedagogic air when writing to him. The present suggestion was more likely to fall on willing ears than another made shortly before their final separation. Atterbury then presented Pope with a Bible, and recommended him to study its pages. If Pope had taken to heart some of St. Paul's exhortations to Christian charity, he would scarcely have published his lines upon Addison, and English literature would have lost some of its most brilliant pages.

Satire of the kind represented by those lines was so obviously adapted to Pope's peculiar talent, that we rather wonder at his having taken to it seriously at a compara-

tively late period, and even then having drifted into it by
accident rather than by deliberate adoption. He had
aimed, as ᵢhas been said, at being a philosophic and
didactic poet. The Essay on Man formed part of a
much larger plan, of which two or three fragmentary
sketches are given by Spence.[1] Bolingbroke and Pope
wrote to Swift in November, 1729, about a scheme then
in course of execution. Bolingbroke declares that Pope
is now exerting what was eminently and peculiarly his
talents, above all writers, living or dead, without except-
ing Horace; whilst Pope explained that this was a "system
of ethics in the Horatian way." The language seems to
apply best to the poems afterwards called the Ethic
Epistles, though, at this time, Pope, perhaps, had not a
very clear plan in his head, and was working at different
parts simultaneously. The Essay on Man, his most
distinct scheme, was to form the opening book of his
poem. Three others were to treat of knowledge and its
limits, of government—ecclesiastical and civil—and of
morality. The last book itself involved an elaborate
plan. There were to be three epistles about each cardinal
virtue—one, for example, upon avarice ; another on the
contrary extreme of prodigality ; and a third, upon the
judicious mean of a moderate use of riches. Pope told
Spence that he had dropped the plan chiefly because his third
book would have provoked every Church on the face of
the earth, and he did not care for always being in boiling
water. The scheme, however, was far too wide and too
systematic for Pope's powers. His spasmodic energy
enabled him only to fill up corners of the canvas, and
from what he did, it is sufficiently evident that his classification would have been incoherent and his philosophy

[1] Spence, pp. 16, 48, 137, 315.

unequal to the task. Part of his work was used for the
fourth book of the Dunciad, and the remainder corresponds to what are now called the Ethic Epistles.
These, as they now stand, include five poems. One of
these has no real connexion with the others. It is a
poem addressed to Addison, " occasioned by his dialogue
on medals," written (according to Pope) in 1715, and
first published in Tickell's edition of Addison's works in
1721. The epistle to Burlington on taste was afterwards
called the Use of Riches, and appended to another with
the same title, thus filling a place in the ethical scheme,
though devoted to a very subsidiary branch of the subject. It appeared in 1731. The epistle " of the use of
riches" appeared in 1732, that of the knowledge and
characters of men in 1733, and that of the characters
of women in 1735. The last three are all that would
seem to belong to the wider treatise contemplated ; but
Pope composed so much in fragments that it is difficult
to say what bits he might have originally intended for any
given purpose.

Another distraction seems to have done more than his
fear of boiling water to arrest the progress of the
elaborate plan. Bolingbroke coming one day into his
room, took up a Horace, and observed that the first satire
of the second book would suit Pope's style. Pope translated it in a morning or two, and sent it to press almost
immediately (1733). The poem had a brilliant success.
It contained, amongst other things, the couplet which
provoked his war with Lady Mary and Lord Hervey.
This, again, led to his putting together the epistle to
Arbuthnot, which includes the bitter attack upon Hervey,
as part of a general *apologia pro vita sua*. It was afterwards called the Prologue to the Satires. Of his other

imitations of Horace, one appeared in 1734 (the second satire of the second book), and four more (the first and sixth epistles of the first book and the first and second of the second book) in 1738.   Finally, in 1737, he published two dialogues, first called " 1738 " and afterwards " The Epilogue to the Satires," which are in the same vein as the epistle to Arbuthnot.   These epistles and imitations of Horace, with the so-called prologue and epilogue, took up the greatest part of Pope's energy during the years in which his intellect was at its best, and show his finest technical qualities.   The Essay on Man was on hand during the early part of this period, the epistles and satires representing a ramification from the same inquiry. But the essay shows the weak side of Pope, whilst his most remarkable qualities are best represented by these subsidiary writings.   The reason will be sufficiently apparent after a brief examination, which will also give occasion for saying what still remains to be said in regard to Pope as a literary artist.

The weakness already conspicuous in the Essay on Man mars the effect of the Ethic Epistles.   His work tends to be rather an aggregation than an organic whole. He was (if I may borrow a phrase from the philologists) an agglutinative writer, and composed by sticking together independent fragments.   His mode of composition was natural to a mind incapable of sustained and continuous thought.   In the epistles, he professes to be working on a plan.   The first expounds his favourite theory (also treated in the essay) of a " ruling passion."   Each man has such a passion, if only you can find it, which explains the apparent inconsistency of his conduct.   This theory, which has exposed him to a charge of fatalism (especially from people who did not very well know what fatalism means), is sufficiently striking for his purpose; but it rather turns up at intervals than really binds the epistle into a whole. But the arrangement of his portrait gallery is really unsystematic; the affectation of system is rather in the way. The most striking characters in the essay on women were inserted (whenever composed) some time after its first appearance, and the construction is too loose to make any interruption of the argument perceptible. The poems contain some of Pope's most brilliant bits, but we can scarcely remember them as a whole. The characters of Wharton and Villiers, of Atossa, of the Man of Ross, and Sir Balaam, stand out as brilliant passages which would do almost as well in any other setting. In the imitations of Horace he is, of course, guided by lines already laid down for him; and he has shown admirable skill in translating the substance as well as the words of his author by the nearest equivalents. This peculiar mode of imitation had been tried by other writers, but in Pope's hands it succeeded beyond all precedent. There is so much congeniality between Horace and Pope, and the social orders of which they were the spokesmen, that he can represent his original without giving us any sense of constraint. Yet even here he sometimes obscures the thread of connexion, and we feel more or less clearly that the order of thought is not that which would have spontaneously arisen in his own mind. So, for example, in the imitation of Horace's first epistle of the first book, the references to the Stoical and Epicurean morals imply a connexion of ideas to which nothing corresponds in Pope's reproduction. Horace is describing a genuine experience, while Pope is only putting together a string of commonplaces. The most interesting part of these imitations are those in which Pope takes advantage of the

suggestions in Horace to be thoroughly autobiographical.
He manages to run his own experience and feelings into
the moulds provided for him by his predecessor. One
of the happiest passages is that in which he turns the
serious panegyric on Augustus into a bitter irony against
the other Augustus, whose name was George, and who,
according to Lord Hervey, was so contrasted with
his prototype, that whereas personal courage was the
one weak point of the emperor, it was the one strong
point of the English king. As soon as Pope has a
chance of expressing his personal antipathies or (to do him
bare justice) his personal attachments, his lines begin to
glow. When he is trying to preach, to be ethical and
philosophical, he is apt to fall into mouthing and to lose
his place; but when he can forget his stilts, or point his
morality by some concrete and personal instance, every
word is alive. And it is this which makes the epilogues,
and more especially the prologue to the satires, his most
impressive performances. The unity which is very ill-
supplied by some ostensible philosophical thesis, or even
by the leading strings of Horace, is given by his own
intense interest in himself. The best way of learning to
enjoy Pope is to get by heart the epistle to Arbuthnot.
That epistle is, as I have said, his Apologia. In its some
400 lines, he has managed to compress more of his feelings and thoughts than would fill an ordinary autobio-
graphy. It is true that the epistle requires a commentator. It wants some familiarity with the events of Pope's
life, and many lines convey only a part of their meaning
unless we are familiar not only with the events, but with
the characters of the persons mentioned. Passages over
which we pass carelessly at the first reading then come
out with wonderful freshness, and single phrases throw a

sudden light upon hidden depths of feeling. It is also
true, unluckily, that parts of it must be read by the
rule of contraries. They tell us not what Pope really
was, but what he wished others to think him, and what
he probably endeavoured to persuade himself that he was.
How far he succeeded in imposing upon himself is indeed
a very curious question which can never be fully answered.
There is the strangest mixture of honesty and hypocrisy.
Let me, he says, live my own and die so too—

> (To live and die is all I have to do)
> Maintain a poet's dignity and ease,
> And see what friends and read what books I please !

Well, he was independent in his fashion, and we can at
least believe that he so far believed in himself. But
when he goes on to say that he " can sleep without a poem
in his head,

> Nor know if Dennis be alive or dead,"

we remember his calling up the maid four times a night
in the dreadful winter of 1740 to save a thought, and the
features writhing in anguish as he read a hostile pamphlet. Presently he informs us that " he thinks a lie in
prose or verse the same "—only too much the same ! and
that " if he pleased, he pleased by manly ways." Alas !
for the manliness. And yet again when he speaks of his
parents,

> Unspotted names and venerable long
> If there be force in virtue or in song,

can we doubt that he is speaking from the heart? We
should perhaps like to forget that the really exquisite and
touching lines in which he speaks of his mother had been
so carefully elaborated.

> Me let the tender office long engage
> To rock the cradle of declining age,

> With lenient acts extend a mother's breath,
> Make languor smile and smooth the bed of death,
> Explore the thought, explain the asking eye,
> And keep awhile one parent from the sky!

If there are more tender and exquisitely expressed lines
in the language, I know not where to find them; and yet
again I should be glad not to be reminded by a cruel
commentator that poor Mrs. Pope had been dead for
two years when they were published, and that even
this touching effusion has therefore a taint of dramatic
affectation.

To me, I confess, it seems most probable, though at
first sight incredible, that these utterances were thoroughly
sincere for the moment. I fancy that under Pope's
elaborate masks of hypocrisy and mystification there was
a heart always abnormally sensitive. Unfortunately it was
as capable of bitter resentment as of warm affection, and
was always liable to be misled by the suggestions of his
strangely irritable vanity. And this seems to me to give
the true key to Pope's poetical as well as to his personal
characteristics.

To explain either, we must remember that he was a man
of impulses; at one instant a mere incarnate thrill of
gratitude or generosity, and in the next of spite or jealousy.
A spasm of wounded vanity would make him for the time
as mean and selfish as other men are made by a frenzy of
bodily fear. He would instinctively snatch at a lie even
when a moment's reflection would have shown that the
plain truth would be more convenient, and therefore he
had to accumulate lie upon lie, each intended to patch up
some previous blunder. Though nominally the poet of
reason, he was the very antithesis of the man who is
reasonable in the highest sense: who is truthful in word

and deed because his conduct is regulated by harmonious
and invariable principles.   Pope was governed by the
instantaneous feeling.   His emotion came in sudden jets
and gushes, instead of a continuous stream.   The same
peculiarity deprives his poetry of continuous harmony or
profound unity of conception.   His lively sense of form
and proportion enables him indeed to fill up a simple
framework (generally of borrowed design) with an eye to
general effect, as in the Rape of the Lock or the first
Dunciad.   But even there his flight is short ; and when
a poem should be governed by the evolution of some profound principle or complex mood of sentiment, he becomes
incoherent and perplexed.   But on the other hand he
can perceive admirably all that can be seen at a glance
from a single point of view.   Though he could not be
continuous, he could return again and again to the same
point ; he could polish, correct, eliminate superfluities,
and compress his meaning more and more closely, till he
has constructed short passages of imperishable excellence.
This microscopic attention to fragments sometimes injures
the connexion, and often involves a mutilation of construction.   He corrects and prunes too closely.   He could,
he says, in reference to the Essay on Man, put things
more briefly in verse than in prose ; one reason being that
he could take liberties of this kind not permitted in prose
writing.   But the injury is compensated by the singular
terseness and vivacity of his best style.   Scarcely any one,
as is often remarked, has left so large a proportion of
quotable phrases,[1] and, indeed, to the present he survives

[1] To take an obviously uncertain test, I find that in Bartlett's
dictionary of familiar quotations, Shakspeare fills 70 pages ; Milton, 23 ; Pope, 18 ; Wordsworth, 16 ; and Byron, 15.   The rest
are nowhere.

chiefly by the current coinage of that kind which bears his image and superscription.

This familiar remark may help us to solve the old problem whether Pope was, or rather in what sense he was, a poet. Much of his work may be fairly described as rhymed prose, differing from prose not in substance or tone of feeling, but only in the form of expression. Every poet has an invisible audience, as an orator has a visible one, who deserve a great part of the merit of his works. Some men may write for the religious or philosophic recluse, and therefore utter the emotions which come to ordinary mortals in the rare moments when the music of the spheres, generally drowned by the din of the commonplace world, becomes audible to their dull senses. Pope, on the other hand, writes for the wits who never listen to such strains, and moreover writes for their ordinary moods. He aims at giving us the refined and doubly distilled essence of the conversation of the statesmen and courtiers of his time. The standard of good writing always implicitly present to his mind is the fitness of his poetry to pass muster when shown by Gay to his duchess, or read after dinner to a party composed of Swift, Bolingbroke, and Congreve. That imaginary audience is always looking over his shoulder, applauding a good hit, chuckling over allusions to the last bit of scandal, and ridiculing any extravagance tending to romance or sentimentalism.

The limitations imposed by such a condition are obvious. As men of taste, Pope's friends would make their bow to the recognized authorities. They would praise *Paradise Lost*, but a new Milton would be as much out of place with them as the real Milton at the court of Charles II. They would really prefer to have his verses tagged by Dryden, or the Samson polished by Pope. They would have ridiculed Wordsworth's mysticism or Shelley's idealism, as they laughed at the religious "enthusiasm" of Law or Wesley, or the metaphysical subtleties of Berkeley and Hume. They preferred the philosophy of the Essay on Man, which might be appropriated by a common-sense preacher, or the rhetoric of *Eloisa and Abelard,* bits of which might be used to excellent effect (as indeed Pope himself used the peroration) by a fine gentleman addressing his gallantry to a contemporary Sappho. It is only too easy to expose their shallowness, and therefore to overlook what was genuine in their feelings. After all, Pope's eminent friends were no mere tailor's blocks for the display of laced coats. Swift and Bolingbroke were not enthusiasts nor philosophers, but certainly they were no fools. They liked in the first place thorough polish. They could appreciate a perfectly turned phrase, an epigram which concentrated into a couplet a volume of quick observations, a smart saying from Rochefoucauld or La Bruyère, which gave an edge to worldly wisdom ; a really brilliant utterance of one of those maxims, half true and not over profound, but still presenting one aspect of life as they saw it, which have since grown rather threadbare. This sort of moralizing, which is the staple of Pope's epistles upon the ruling passion or upon avarice, strikes us now as unpleasantly obvious. We have got beyond it and want some more refined analysis and more complex psychology. Take, for example, Pope's epistle to Bathurst, which was in hand for two years, and is just 400 lines in length. The simplicity of the remarks is almost comic. Nobody wants to be told now that bribery is facilitated by modern system of credit.

> Blest paper-credit ! last and best supply
> That lends corruption lighter wings to fly !

This triteness blinds us to the singular felicity with
which the observations have been versified, a felicity which
makes many of the phrases still proverbial. The mark is
so plain that we do scant justice to the accuracy and precision with which it is hit. Yet when we notice how
every epithet tells, and how perfectly the writer does what
he tries to do, we may understand why Pope extorted
contemporary admiration. We may, for example, read once
more the familiar passage about Buckingham. The
picture, such as it is, could not be drawn more strikingly
with fewer lines.

> In the worst inn's worst room, with mat half-hung,
> The floors of plaister and the walls of dung,
> On once a flock-bed but repair'd with straw,
> With tape-ty'd curtains never meant to draw,
> The George and Garter dangling from that bed,
> Where tawdry yellow strove with dirty red,
> Great Villiers lies! alas, how changed from him,
> That life of pleasure and that soul of whim!
> Gallant and gay in Cliveden's proud alcove,
> The bower of wanton Shrewsbury and love;
> As great as gay, at council in a ring
> Of mimick'd statesmen, and their merry king.
> No wit to flatter left of all his store!
> No fool to laugh at, which he valued more.
> Thus, victor of his health, of fortune, friends,
> And fame, the lord of useless thousands ends.

It is as graphic as a page of Dickens, and has the advantage of being less grotesque, if the sentiment is equally
obvious. When Pope has made his hit, he does not blur
the effect by trying to repeat it.

In these epistles, it must be owned that the sentiment
is not only obvious but prosaic. The moral maxims are
delivered like advice offered by one sensible man to
another, not with the impassioned fervour of a prophet,

Nor can Pope often rise to that level at which alone satire is transmuted into the higher class of poetry. To accomplish that feat, if, indeed, it be possible, the poet must not simply ridicule the fantastic tricks of poor mortals, but show how they appear to the angels who weep over them. The petty figures must be projected against a background of the infinite, and we must feel the relations of our tiny eddies of life to the oceanic currents of human history. Pope can never rise above the crowd. He is looking at his equals, not contemplating them from the height which reveals their insignificance. The element, which may fairly be called poetical, is derived from an inferior source; but sometimes has passion enough in it to lift him above mere prose.

In one of his most animated passages, Pope relates his desire to—

> Brand the bold front of shameless guilty men.
> Dash the proud gamester in his gilded car,
> Bare the mean heart that lurks beneath a star.

For the moment he takes himself seriously; and, indeed, he seems to have persuaded both himself and his friends that he was really a great defender of virtue. Arbuthnot begged him, almost with his dying breath, to continue his "noble disdain and abhorrence of vice," and, with a due regard to his own safety, to try rather to reform than chastise; and Pope accepts the office ostentatiously. His provocation is "the strong antipathy of good to bad," and he exclaims,—

> Yes! I am proud—I must be proud to see
> Men not afraid of God, afraid of me.
> Safe from the bar, the pulpit, and the throne,
> Yet touch'd and shamed by ridicule alone.

If the sentiment provokes a slight incredulity, it is yet

worth while to understand its real meaning; and the explanation is not very far to seek.

Pope's best writing, I have said, is the essence of conversation. It has the quick movement, the boldness and brilliance, which we suppose to be the attributes of the best talk. Of course the apparent facility is due to conscientious labour. In the Prologue and Epilogue and the best parts of the imitations of Horace, he shows such consummate mastery of his peculiar style, that we forget the monotonous metre. The opening passage, for example, of the Prologue is written apparently with the perfect freedom of real dialogue; in fact, it is of course far more pointed and compressed than any dialogue could ever be. The dramatic vivacity with which the whole scene is given, shows that he could use metre as the most skilful performer could command a musical instrument. Pope, indeed, shows in the Essay on Criticism, that his view about the uniformity of sound and sense were crude enough; they are analogous to the tricks by which a musician might decently imitate the cries of animals or the murmurs of a crowd; and his art excludes any attempt at rivalling the melody of the great poets who aim at producing a harmony quite independent of the direct meaning of their words. I am only speaking of the felicity with which he can move in metre, without the slightest appearance of restraint, so as to give a kind of idealized representation of the tone of animated verbal intercourse. Whatever comes within this province he can produce with admirable fidelity. Now in such talks as we imagine with Swift and Bolingbroke, we may be quite sure that there would be some very forcible denunciation of corruption—corruption being of course regarded as due to the diabolical agency of Walpole. During his later years,

Pope became a friend of all the Opposition clique, which
was undermining the power of the great minister. In his
last letters to Swift, Pope speaks of the new circle of
promising patriots who were rising round him, and from
whom he entertained hopes of the regeneration of this
corrupt country.   Sentiments of this kind were the staple
talk of the circles in which he moved ; and all the young
men of promise believed, or persuaded themselves to fancy,
that a political millennium would follow the downfall of
Walpole.   Pope, susceptible as always to the influences of
his social surroundings, took in all this, and delighted in
figuring himself as the prophet of the new era and the
denouncer of wickedness in high places.   He sees " old
England's genius " dragged in the dust, hears the black
trumpet of vice proclaiming that " not to be corrupted is
the shame," and declares that he will draw the last pen
for freedom, and use his " sacred weapon " in truth's
defence.

To imagine Pope at his best, we must place ourselves in
Twickenham on some fine day, when the long disease
has relaxed its grasp for a moment ; when he has taken a
turn through his garden, and comforted his poor frame with
potted lampreys and a glass or two from his frugal pint.
Suppose two or three friends to be sitting with him, the
stately Bolingbroke or the mercurial Bathurst, with one of
the patriotic hopes of mankind, Marchmont or Lyttelton,
to stimulate his ardour, and the amiable Spence, or Mrs.
Patty Blount to listen reverentially to his morality.   Let
the conversation kindle into vivacity, and host and guests
fall into a friendly rivalry, whetting each other's wits by
lively repartee, and airing the little fragments of worldly
wisdom which pass muster for profound observation at
Court ; for a time they talk platitudes, though striking

out now and then brilliant flashes, as from the collision of
polished rapiers ; they diverge, perhaps, into literature, and
Pope shines in discussing the secrets of the art to which
his whole life has been devoted with untiring fidelity.
Suddenly the mention of some noted name provokes a
startling outburst of personal invective from Pope ; his
friends judiciously divert the current of wrath into a new
channel, and he becomes for the moment a generous patriot
declaiming against the growth of luxury ; the mention of
some sympathizing friend brings out a compliment, so exquisitely turned, as to be a permanent title of honour,
conferred by genius instead of power; or the thought of
his parents makes his voice tremble, and his eyes shine
with pathetic softness ; and you forgive the occasional
affectation which you can never quite forget, or even the
occasional grossness or harshness of sentiment which contrasts so strongly with the superficial polish.   A genuine
report of even the best conversation would be intolerably
prosy and unimaginative.   But imagine the very pith and
essence of such talk brought to a focus, concentrated into
the smallest possible space with the infinite dexterity of a
thoroughly trained hand, and you have the kind of writing
in which Pope is unrivalled ; polished prose with occasional gleams of genuine poetry—the epistle to Arbuthnot
and the epilogue to the Satires.

One point remains to be briefly noticed.   The virtue
on which Pope prided himself was correctness ; and I
have interpreted this to mean the quality which is gained
by incessant labour, guided by quick feeling, and always
under the strict supervision of common sense.   The next
literary revolution led to a depreciation of this quality.
Warton (like Macaulay long afterwards) argued that in
a higher sense, the Elizabethan poets were really as correct

as Pope.   Their poetry embodied a higher and more complex law, though it neglected the narrow cut-and-dried
precepts recognized in the Queen Anne period.   The new
school came to express too undiscriminating a contempt
for the whole theory and practice of Pope and his followers.   Pope, said Cowper, and a thousand critics have
echoed his words,—

> Made poetry a mere mechanic art
> And every warbler had his tune by heart.

Without discussing the wider question, I may here
briefly remark that this judgment, taken absolutely, gives
a very false impression of Pope's artistic quality.   Pope
is undoubtedly monotonous.   Except in one or two lyrics,
such as the Ode on St. Cecilia's Day, which must be
reckoned amongst his utter failures, he invariably employed
the same metre.   The discontinuity of his style, and the
strict rules which he adopted, tend to disintegrate his
poems.   They are a series of brilliant passages, often of
brilliant couplets, stuck together in a conglomerate ; and
as the inferior connecting matter decays, the interstices open
and allow the whole to fall into ruin.   To read a series of
such couplets, each complete in itself, and each so constructed as to allow of a very small variety of form, is
naturally to receive an impression of monotony.   Pope's
antitheses fall into a few common forms, which are repeated over and over again, and seem copy to each other.
And, in a sense, such work can be very easily imitated.
A very inferior artist can obtain most of his efforts, and all
the external qualities of his style.   One ten-syllabled
rhyming couplet, with the whole sense strictly confined
within its limits, and allowing only of such variety as
follows from changing the pauses, is undoubtedly very

much like another. And accordingly one may read in
any collection of British poets innumerable pages of verifi-
cation which—if you do not look too close—are exactly like
Pope. All poets who have any marked style are more or
less imitable ; in the present age of revivals, a clever
versifier is capable of adopting the manners of his leading
contemporaries, or that of any poet from Spenser to
Shelley or Keats. The quantity of work scarcely dis-
tinguishable from that of the worst passages in Mr. Ten-
nyson, Mr. Browning, and Mr. Swinburne, seems to be
limited only by the supply of stationery at the disposal of
practised performers. That which makes the imitations of
Pope prominent is partly the extent of his sovereignty ; the
vast number of writers who confined themselves exclusively
to his style ; and partly the fact that what is easily imitable
in him is so conspicuous an element of the whole. The
rigid framework which he adopted is easily definable
with mathematical precision. The difference between the
best work of Pope and the ordinary work of his followers
is confined within narrow limits, and not easily perceived
at a glance. The difference between blank verse in the
hands of its few masters and in the hands of a third-rate
imitator strikes the ear in every line. Far more is left
to the individual idiosyncrasy. But it does not at all
follow, and in fact it is quite untrue that the distinction
which turns on an apparently insignificant element is
therefore unimportant. The value of all good work
ultimately depends on touches so fine as to elude the
sight. And the proof is that although Pope was so constantly imitated, no later and contemporary writer succeeded in approaching his excellence. Young, of the
Night Thoughts, was an extraordinarily clever writer and
talker, even if he did not (as one of his hearers asserts)

eclipse Voltaire by the brilliance of his conversation, Young's satires show abundance of wit, and one may not be able to say at a glance in what they are inferior to Pope. Yet they have hopelessly perished, whilst Pope's work remains classical. Of all the crowd of eighteenth-century writers in Pope's manner, only two made an approach to him worth notice. Johnson's *Vanity of Human Wishes* surpasses Pope in general sense of power, and Goldsmith's two poems in the same style have phrases of a higher order than Pope's. But even these poems have not made so deep a mark. In the last generation, Gifford's *Baviad and Mæviad*, and Byron's *English Bards and Scotch Reviewers*, were clever reproductions of the manner ; but Gifford is already unreadable, and Byron is pale beside his original ; and, therefore, making full allowance for Pope's monotony, and the tiresome prominence of certain mechanical effects, we must, I think, admit that he has after all succeeded in doing with unsurpassable excellence what innumerable rivals have failed to do as well. The explanation is—if the phrase explains anything—that he was a man of genius, or that he brought to a task, not of the highest class, a keenness of sensibility, a conscientious desire to do his very best, and a capacity for taking pains with his work, which enabled him to be as indisputably the first in his own peculiar line, as our greatest men have been in far more lofty undertakings.

The man who could not publish Pastorals without getting into quarrels, was hardly likely to become a professed satirist without giving offence. Besides numerous stabs administered to old enemies, Pope opened some fresh animosities by passages in these poems. Some pointed ridicule was aimed at Montagu, Earl of Halifax, in the Prologue ; for there can be no doubt that Halifax [3] was pointed out in the character of Bufo. Pope told a story in later days of an introduction to Halifax, the great patron of the early years of the century, who wished to hear him read his Homer. After the reading Halifax suggested that one passage should be improved. Pope retired rather puzzled by his vague remarks, but, by Garth's advice, returned some time afterwards, and read the same passage without alteration. "Ay, now Mr. Pope," said Halifax, "they are perfectly right ; nothing can be better !" This little incident perhaps suggested to Pope that Halifax was a humbug, and there seems, as already noticed, to have been some difficulty about the desired dedication of the Iliad. Though Halifax had been dead for twenty years when the Prologue appeared, Pope may have been in the right in satirizing the pompous would-be patron, from whom he had received nothing, and whose pretences he had seen through. But the bitterness of the attack is disagreeable when we add that Pope paid Halifax high compliments in the preface to the Iliad, and boasted of his friendship, shortly after the satire, in the Epilogue to the Satires. A more disagreeable affair at the moment was the description, in the Epistle on Taste, of Canons, the splendid seat of the Duke of Chandos. Chandos, being still alive, resented the attack, and Pope had not the courage to avow his meaning, which might in that case have been justifiable. He declared to Burlington (to whom the epistle was addressed), and to Chandos, that he had not intended Canons, and tried to make peace by saying in another epistle that " gracious Chandos is beloved at sight." This exculpation, says John-

---

[3] Roscoe's attempt at a denial was conclusively answered by Bowles in one of his pamphlets.

son, was received by the duke "with great magnanimity, as by a man who accepted his excuse, without believing his professions." Nobody, in fact, believed, and even Warburton let out the secret by a comic oversight. Pope had prophesied in his poem that another age would see the destruction of "Timon's Villa," when laughing Ceres would reassume the land. Had he lived three years longer, said Warburton in a note, Pope would have seen his prophecy fulfilled, namely, by the destruction of Canons. The note was corrected, but the admission that Canons belonged to Timon had been made.

To such accusations Pope had a general answer. He described the type, not the individual. The fault was with the public, who chose to fit the cap. His friend remonstrates in the Epilogue against his personal satire. "Come on, then, Satire, general, unconfined," exclaims the poet,

> Spread thy broad wing and souse on all the kind.
> *   *   *   *   *
> Ye reverend atheists. (Friend) Scandal! name them! who?
> (Pope) Why, that's the thing you bade me not to do.
> Who starved a sister, who forswore a debt,
> I never named; the town's inquiring yet.
> The pois'ning dame— (F.) You mean— (P.) I don't.
>   (F.) You do.
> (P.) See, now, I keep the secret, and not you!

It must in fact be admitted that from the purely artistic point of view, Pope is right. Prosaic commentators are always asking, Who is meant by a poet, as though a poem were a legal document. It may be interesting, for various purposes, to know who was in the writer's mind, or what fact suggested the general picture. But we have no right to look outside the poem itself, or to infer anything not within the four corners of the statement. It matters not for such purposes whether there was, or was not, any real person corresponding to Sir Balaam, to whom his wife said, when he was enriched by Cornish wreckers, "live like yourself,"

When lo! two puddings smoked upon the board,

in place of the previous one on Sabbath days. Nor does it even matter whether Atticus meant Addison, or Sappho Lady Mary. The satire is equally good, whether its objects are mere names or realities.

But the moral question is quite distinct. In that case we must ask whether Pope used words calculated or intended to fix an imputation upon particular people. Whether he did it in prose or verse, the offence was the same. In many cases he gives real names, and in many others gives unmistakable indications, which must have fixed his satire to particular people. If he had written Addison for Atticus (as he did at first), or Lady Mary for Sappho, or Halifax for Bufo, the insinuation could not have been clearer. His attempt to evade his responsibility was a mere equivocation—a device which he seems to have preferred to direct lying. The character of Bufo might be equally suitable to others; but no reasonable man could doubt that every one would fix it upon Halifax. In some cases—possibly in that of Chandos—he may have thought that his language was too general to apply, and occasionally it seems that he sometimes tried to evade consequences by adding some inconsistent characteristic to his portraits.

I say this, because I am here forced to notice the worst of all the imputations upon Pope's character. The epistle on the characters of women now includes the famous lines on Atossa, which did not appear till after Pope's death.[4] They were (in 1746) at once applied to the famous Sarah, Duchess of Marlborough ; and a story immediately became current that the duchess had paid Pope 1000*l.* to suppress them, but that he preserved them, with a view to their ultimate publication. This story was repeated by Warton and by Walpole ; it has been accepted by Mr. Carruthers, who suggests, by way of palliation, that Pope was desirous at the time of providing for Martha Blount, and probably took the sum in order to buy an annuity for her. Now, if the story were proved, it must be admitted that it would reveal a baseness in Pope which would be worthy only of the lowest and most venal literary marauders. No more disgraceful imputation could have been made upon Curll, or Curll's miserable dependents. A man who could so prostitute his talents must have been utterly vile. Pope has sins enough to answer for ; but his other meannesses were either sacrifices to his morbid vanity, or (like his offence against Swift, or his lies to Aaron Hill and Chandos) collateral results of spasmodic attempts to escape from humiliation. In money-matters he seems to have been generally independent. He refused gifts from his rich friends, and confuted the rather similar calumny that he had received 500*l.* from the Duke of Chandos. If the account rested upon mere contemporary scandal, we might reject it on the ground of its inconsistency with his known character, and its likeness to other fabrications of his enemies. There is, however, further evidence. It is such evidence as would, at most, justify a verdict of "not proven" in a court of justice. But the critic is not bound by legal rules, and has to say what is the most probable solution, without fear or favour.

I cannot here go into the minute details. This much,

[4] On this subject Mr. Dilke's *Papers of a Critic.*

however, may be taken as established. Pope was printing
a new edition of his works at the time of his death. He
had just distributed to his friends some copies of the
Ethic Epistles, and in those copies the Atossa appeared.
Bolingbroke, to whom Pope had left his unpublished
papers, discovered it, and immediately identified it with
the duchess, who (it must be noticed) was still alive. He
wrote to Marchmont, one of Pope's executors, that there
could be "no excuse for Pope's design of publishing it
after the favour you and I know." This is further
explained by a note added in pencil by Marchmont's
executor, "1000l. ;" and the son of this executor, who published the Marchmont papers, says that this was the favour
received by Pope from the duchess. This, however, is
far from proving a direct bribe. It is, in fact, hardly
conceivable that the duchess and Pope should have made
such a bargain in direct black and white, and equally inconceivable that two men like Bolingbroke and Marchmont should have been privy to such a transaction, and
spoken of it in such terms. Bolingbroke thinks that the
favour received laid Pope under an obligation, but evidently does not think that it implied a contract. Mr. Dilke
has further pointed out that there are many touches in the
character which distinctly apply to the Duchess of Buckingham, with whom Pope had certainly quarrelled, and
which will not apply to the Duchess of Marlborough,
who had undoubtedly made friends with him during the
last years of his life. Walpole again tells a story, partly
confirmed by Warton, that Pope had shown the character to each duchess (Warton says only to Marlborough), saying that it was meant for the other. The
Duchess of Buckingham, he says, believed him; the other
had more sense and paid him 1000l. to suppress it.

Walpole is no trustworthy authority ; but the coincidence implies at least that such a story was soon current.

The most probable solution must conform to these data. Pope's Atossa was a portrait which would fit either lady, though it would be naturally applied to the most famous. It seems certain also that Pope had received some favours (possibly the 1000*l.* on some occasion unknown) from the Duchess of Marlborough, which was felt by his friends to make any attack upon her unjustifiable. We can scarcely believe that there should have been a direct compact of the kind described. If Pope had been a person of duly sensitive conscience he would have suppressed his work. But to suppress anything that he had written, and especially a passage so carefully laboured, was always agony to him. He preferred, as we may perhaps conjecture, to settle in his own mind that it would fit the Duchess of Buckingham, and possibly introduced some of the touches to which Mr. Dilke refers. He thought it sufficiently disguised to be willing to publish it whilst the person with whom it was naturally identified was still alive. Had she complained, he would have relied upon those touches, and have equivocated as he equivocated to Hill and Chandos. He always seems to have fancied that he could conceal himself by very thin disguises. But he ought to have known, and perhaps did know, that it would be immediately applied to the person who had conferred an obligation. From that guilt no hypothesis can relieve him ; but it is certainly not proved, and seems, on the whole, improbable that he was so base as the concessions of his biographers would indicate.

CHAPTER IX.

THE END.

THE last satires were published in 1738. Six years of life
still remained to Pope; his intellectual powers were still
vigorous, and his pleasure in their exercise had not ceased.
The only fruit, however, of his labours during this period
was the fourth book of the Dunciad. He spent much
time upon bringing out new editions of his works, and
upon the various intrigues connected with the Swift correspondence. But his health was beginning to fail. The
ricketty framework was giving way, and failing to answer
the demands of the fretful and excitable brain. In the
spring of 1744 the poet was visibly breaking up; he
suffered from dropsical asthma, and seems to have made
matters worse by putting himself in the hands of a notorious quack—a Dr. Thomson. The end was evidently near
as he completed his fifty-sixth year. Friends, old and
new, were often in attendance. Above all, Bolingbroke,
the venerated friend of thirty years' standing; Patty
Blount, the woman whom he loved best; and the excellent Spence, who preserved some of the last words of the
dying man. The scene, as he saw it, was pathetic;
perhaps it is not less pathetic to us, for whom it has
another side as of grim tragic humour.

Three weeks before his death Pope was sending off

copies of the Ethic Epistles—apparently with the Atossa lines—to his friends. " Here I am, like Socrates," he said, " dispensing my morality amongst my friends just as I am dying." Spence watched him as anxiously as his disciples watched Socrates. He was still sensible to kindness. Whenever Miss Blount came in, the failing spirits rallied for a moment. He was always saying something kindly of his friends, " as if his humanity had outlasted his understanding." Bolingbroke, when Spence made the remark, said that he had never known a man with so tender a heart for his own friends or for mankind. " I have known him," he added, " these thirty years, and value myself more for that man's love than—" and his voice was lost in tears. At moments Pope could still be playful. " Here I am, dying of a hundred good symptoms," he replied to some flattering report, but his mind was beginning to wander. He complained of seeing things as through a curtain. " What's that ? " he said, pointing to the air, and then, with a smile of great pleasure, added softly, " 'twas a vision." His religious sentiments still edified his hearers. " I am so certain," he said, " of the soul's being immortal, that I seem to feel it within me, as it were by intuition ;" and early one morning he rose from bed and tried to begin an essay upon immortality, apparently in a state of semi-delirium. On his last day he sacrificed, as Chesterfield rather cynically observes, his cock to Æsculapius. Hooke, a zealous Catholic friend, asked him whether he would not send for a priest. " I do not suppose that it is essential," said Pope, " but it will look right, and I heartily thank you for putting me in mind of it." A priest was brought, and Pope received the last sacraments with great fervour and resignation. Next day, on May 30th, 1744, he died so peacefully that his friends could not determine the exact moment of death.

It was a soft and touching end ; and yet we must once more look at the other side. Warburton and Boling-broke both appear to have been at the side of the dying man, and before very long they were to be quarrelling over his grave. Pope's will showed at once that his quarrels were hardly to end with his death. He had quarrelled, though the quarrel had been made up, with the generous Allen, for some cause not ascertainable, except that it arose from the mutual displeasure of Mrs. Allen and Miss Blount. It is pleasant to notice that, in the course of the quarrel, Pope mentioned Warburton, in a letter to Miss Blount, as a sneaking parson ; but War-burton was not aware of the flash of sarcasm. Pope, as Johnson puts it, " polluted his will with female resent-ment." He left a legacy of 150*l.* to Allen, being, as he added, the amount received from his friend—for himself or for charitable purposes ; and requested Allen, if he should refuse the legacy for himself, to pay it to the Bath Hospital. Allen adopted this suggestion, saying quietly that Pope had always been a bad accountant, and would have come nearer the truth if he had added a cypher to the figures.

Another fact came to light, which produced a fiercer out-burst. Pope, it was found, had printed a whole edition (1500 copies) of the *Patriot King*, Bolingbroke's most polished work. The motive could have been nothing but a desire to preserve to posterity what Pope considered to be a monument worthy of the highest genius, and was so far complimentary to Bolingbroke. Bolingbroke, how-ever, considered it as an act of gross treachery. Pope had received the work on condition of keeping it strictly

private, and showing it to only a few friends. Moreover, he had corrected it, arranged it, and altered or
omitted passages according to his own taste, which naturally did not suit the author's.   In 1749 Bolingbroke
gave a copy to Mallet for publication, and prefixed an
angry statement to expose the breach of trust of "a man
on whom the author thought he could entirely depend."
Warburton rushed to the defence of Pope and the demo-
lition of Bolingbroke. A savage controversy followed,
which survives only in the title of one of Bolingbroke's
pamphlets, A Familiar Epistle to the most Impudent
Man living—a transparent paraphrase for Warburton.
Pope's behaviour is too much of a piece with previous
underhand transactions, but scarcely deserves further con-
demnation.

A single touch remains. Pope was buried, by his own
directions, in a vault in Twickenham church, near the
monument erected to his parents. It contained a simple
inscription ending with the words "*Parentibus bene meren-
tibus filius fecit.*" To this, as he directed in his will,
was to be added simply "*et sibi.*" This was done; but
seventeen years afterwards the clumsy Warburton erected
in the same church another monument to Pope himself,
with this stupid inscription. *Poeta loquitur.*

> *For one who would not be buried in Westminster Abbey.*
> Heroes and kings, your distance keep!
> In peace let one poor poet sleep
> Who never flatter'd folks like you;
> Let Horace blush and Virgil too

Most of us can tell from experience how grievously our
posthumous ceremonials often jar upon the tenderest
feelings of survivors. Pope's valued friends seem to have
done their best to surround the last scene of his life with

P

painful associations; and Pope, alas! was an unconscious accomplice. To us of a later generation it is impossible to close this strange history without a singular mixture of feelings. Admiration for the extraordinary literary talents, respect for the energy which, under all disadvantages of health and position, turned these talents to the best account; love of the real tender-heartedness which formed the basis of the man's character; pity for the many sufferings to which his morbid sensitiveness exposed him; contempt for the meannesses into which he was hurried; ridicule for the insatiable vanity which prompted his most degrading subterfuges; horror for the bitter animosities which must have tortured the man who cherished them even more than his victims—are suggested simultaneously by the name of Pope. As we look at him in one or other aspect, each feeling may come uppermost in turn. The most abiding sentiment—when we think of him as a literary phenomenon—is admiration for the exquisite skill which enabled him to discharge a function, not of the highest kind, with a perfection rare in any department of literature. It is more difficult to say what will be the final element in our feeling about the man. Let us hope that it may be the pity which, after a certain lapse of years, we may be excused for conceding to the victim of moral as well as physical diseases.

THE END.